NORFOLK'S MILITARY HERITAGE

Neil R. Storey

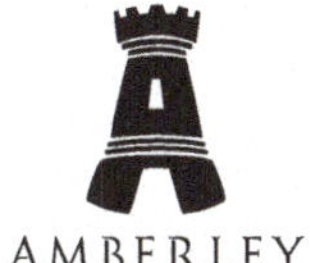

First published 2019

Amberley Publishing
The Hill, Stroud
Gloucestershire, GL5 4EP

www.amberley-books.com

Copyright © Neil R. Storey, 2019

Logo source material courtesy of Gerry van Tonder

The right of Neil R. Storey to be identified as the
Author of this work has been asserted in accordance
with the Copyrights, Designs and Patents Act 1988.

ISBN 978 1 4456 8822 0 (print)
ISBN 978 1 4456 8823 7 (ebook)

British Library Cataloguing in Publication Data.
A catalogue record for this book is available from the
British Library.

Origination by Amberley Publishing.
Printed in Great Britain.

Contents

Introduction   5

1. Echoes of Ancient Conflicts   7

2. Conquerors and Castles   11

3. Revolt, Rebellion and the Spanish Armada   17

4. The English Civil War   21

5. Revolutionary and Napoleonic Wars   25

6. The Victorian and Edwardian Eras   31

7. The First World War   43

8. The Interwar Years   59

9. The Second World War   63

10. The Royal Norfolk Regiment   76

Postscript   93

Acknowledgements   96

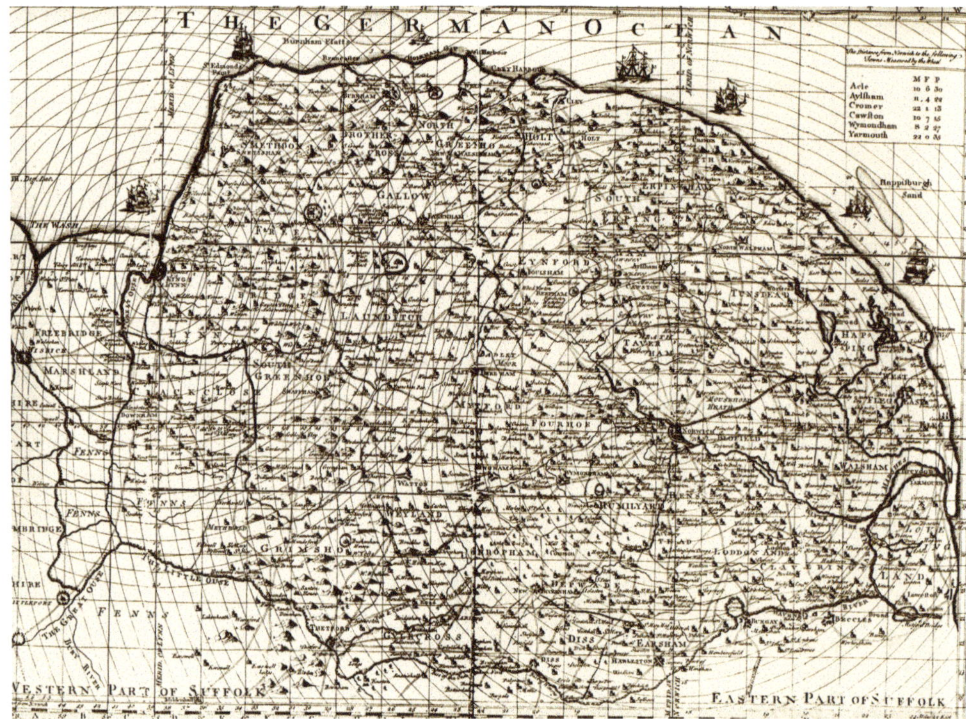

A rare military map of Norfolk, *c.* 1800. Note the men o' war off the coast of the German Ocean (the old name for the North Sea) and the concentric circles radiating from King's Lynn and Norwich to aid the calculation of distances.

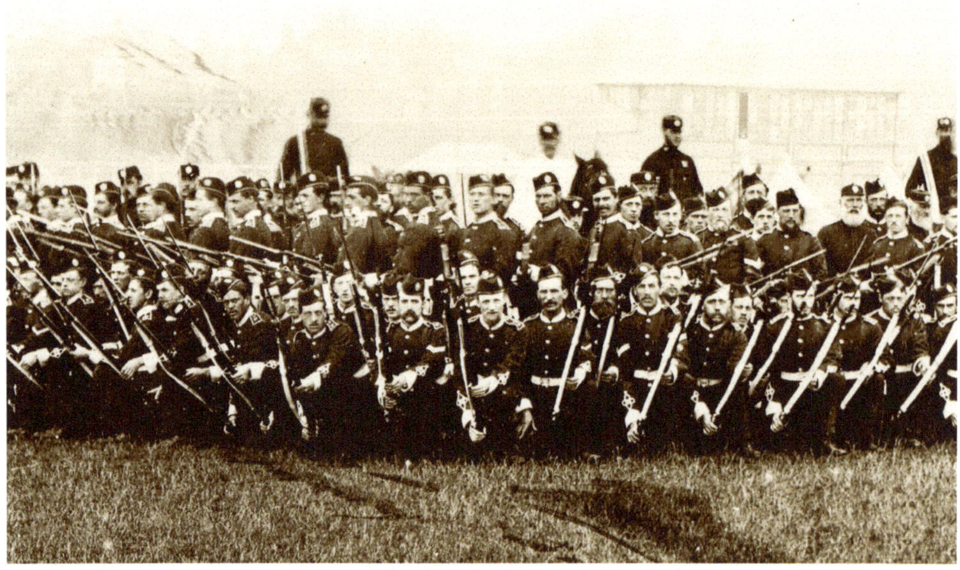

Soldiers of 3rd Norfolk Rifle Volunteers prepare to repel cavalry during a field day on South Denes, Great Yarmouth, 1879.

Introduction

I am myself a Norfolk man and glory in being so.

Admiral Lord Nelson

Norfolk is one of England's largest counties. It still has thousands of acres of rich, fertile agricultural land and has housed human settlements since the earliest times, along with their resulting conflicts. Add to this a coastline stretching nearly 100 miles from the Wash to Hopton-on-Sea, with a number of natural harbours and navigable waterways, and you can see why dear old Norfolk has often been a target for raids and invasions down the centuries.

Perhaps these are some of the reasons why Norfolk people have a natural propensity for standing up for themselves and what they believe is right. Famously, in ancient history the Iceni were led in battle by Queen Boudica in a campaign that almost drove the Roman occupiers out of the British Isles. That fighting spirit remains in our blood, mingled with that of the Saxons, Vikings and Normans.

Norfolk people have risen in rebellion on numerous occasions against oppression and to defend their way of life, notably during the Peasants' Revolt in 1381 and Kett's Rebellion of 1549. Ultimately they faced forces that were larger and far better armed than them, but rise they did, and made their point.

During the English Civil War, despite being predominantly in favour of the Parliamentary cause, both Royalists and Parliamentarians made their stands in the county and many Norfolk men joined regiments that fought in some of the notable actions of the war around the country. Captain Robert Swallow raised the 'Maiden Troop' of Cromwell's Ironside cavalry in Norwich. Norfolk formed part of the Eastern Association that proved to be the backbone of the Parliamentarian forces by late 1644.

Norfolk fighting men have demonstrated their steadfastness and courage in battle again and again, notably through two world wars. Lieutenant General Sir Brian Horrocks summed this up in his special introduction in *Royal Norfolk Regiment* (part of the Famous Regiments series) in which he said:

The Royal Norfolk Regiment has always been renowned for its steadfastness and reliability in difficult situations. In fact it is the sort of Regiment which all commanders like to have available in order to plug a difficult gap. This staunchness has been developed over the years, for wherever the fighting was fiercest, climatic conditions most vile and the odds against victory most daunting, the 9th Foot was sure to be there.

This spirit is also reflected through the service of Norfolk personnel in the Royal Navy, the Royal Air Force and even among those on the home front during dark times, danger and disaster.

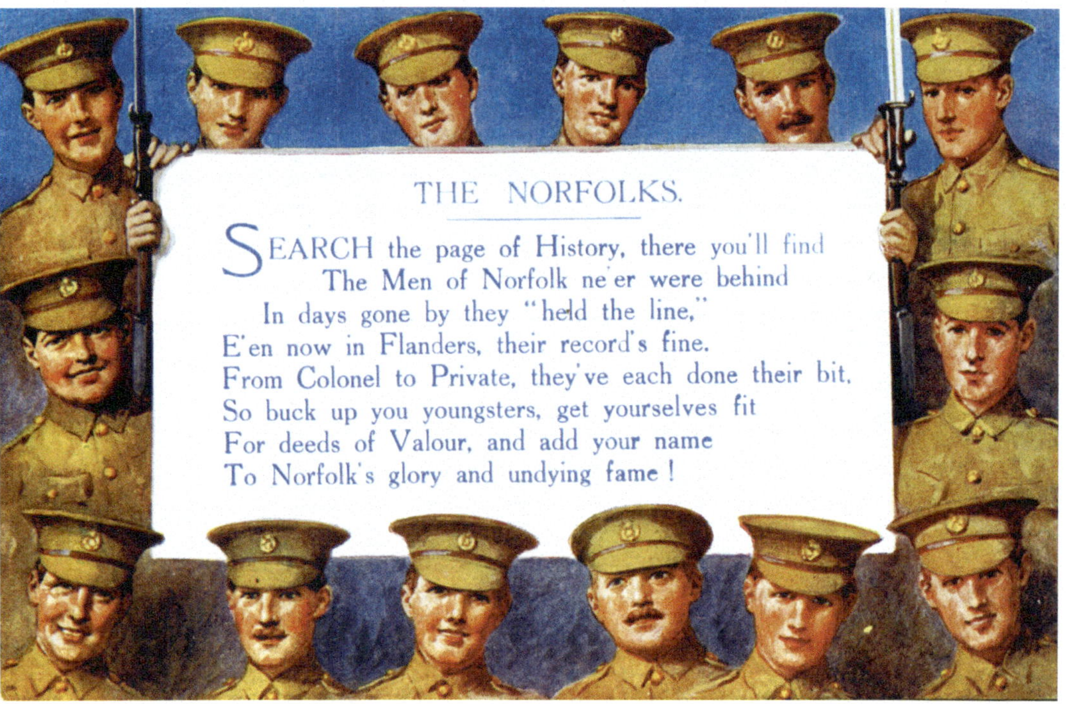

A patriotic postcard paying tribute to the Norfolk Regiment that was produced during the First World War.

Norfolk has been the scene of riots, rebellions, sieges and military action over past centuries and the landscape is dotted with castles, earthworks, defences, moats and fortified manor houses. Some of these are now long gone, revealed only in the fields as crop marks in dry weather; others are ruins and some remain remarkable bastions to this day. This book does not attempt to be encyclopaedic, but I hope it will highlight some of the most interesting places and inspire a visit to those open to the public. Above all I hope it will introduce the story of our local regiments and our military past to anyone with a budding interest in the subject, be they Norfolk born and bred, resident or visitor, and deepen their appreciation of Norfolk's rich military heritage.

Neil R. Storey, 2019

1. Echoes of Ancient Conflicts

The Iceni and the Romans

The rich fertile lands of Norfolk have attracted farming settlements since the earliest of times. During the Iron Age (*c.* 700 BC–AD 43) the iron tools and improved farming methods that developed transformed the county, bringing more land into cultivation and increasing the population. The changing times also saw aggression between rival tribes, who would fight with improved metal weapons to expand their territory and gain control of the best land and resources. Consequently, communities began to create defensive ditches and earthworks – these date from over a 700-year period before the Roman occupation of Britain.

There are five, possibly six, known Iron Age earthwork forts in Norfolk, but there would almost certainly have been more. Sadly many have been lost following demolition and ploughing over the centuries, such as the hill fort at Bloodgate Hill, South Creake, which once commanded views across the Burn Valley and to the sea to the north. Four of the other known hill forts have more discernable ditches and ramparts. Inland, Narborough Fort was built close to the crossing of the River Nar and the ancient Icknield Way, and Thetford Fort (also near the Icknield Way) oversaw the important river crossings of both the Thet and the Ouse.

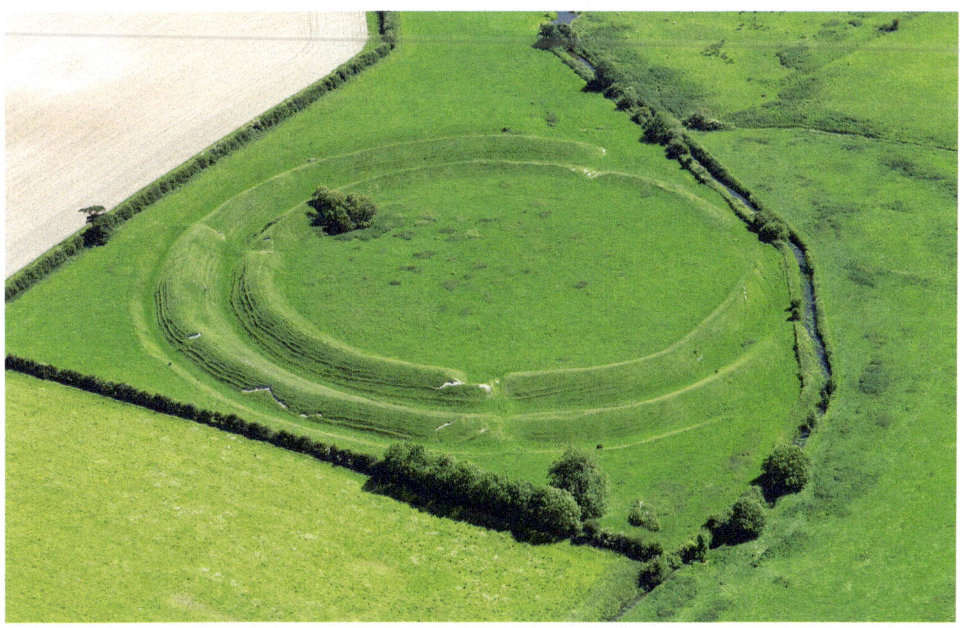

Norfolk's best example of an Iron Age fort at Warham, near Wells. (Courtesy of John Fieldiing)

Near the coast are the lowland forts at Holkham and Warham. Holkham Fort is one of two possible sites (the other being Stonea Camp in Cambridgeshire) that Roman historian Tacitus identified as the scene of the defeat of the first Iceni rebellion by a Roman force, led by Ostorius Scapula in AD 47. Norfolk's best example of an Iron Age fort is at Warham. Circular in construction, it is 212 metres in diameter, enclosing an area of around 1.5 hectares with a 3-metre-high double bank and ditch, and ramparts constructed from chalk rubble. It was undoubtedly built for defence, but whether Holkham and Warham forts were under constant occupation as settlements or predominantly used as places of refuge and defence in the event of an attack is still debated.

Roman Occupation

The Celtic tribe of the Iceni held the majority of East Anglia at the time of the Roman invasion in AD 43 and had agreed favourable terms with the officials of Emperor Claudius. After the death of the Iceni King Presutagus in AD 61, the new Roman Emperor Nero refused to renew the terms. In the dispute that followed, the king's widow, Boudica, was publicly beaten by Roman soldiers and her daughters raped. Insulted at their treatment, the Iceni rose in revolt led by Queen Boudica. The uprising stormed and burned Camulodunum (Colchester), Londinium (London) and Verulamium (St Albans). It was so successful that Nero considered withdrawing Roman forces from Britain, but the Roman army under Suetonius Paulinus eventually gained the upper hand and crushed

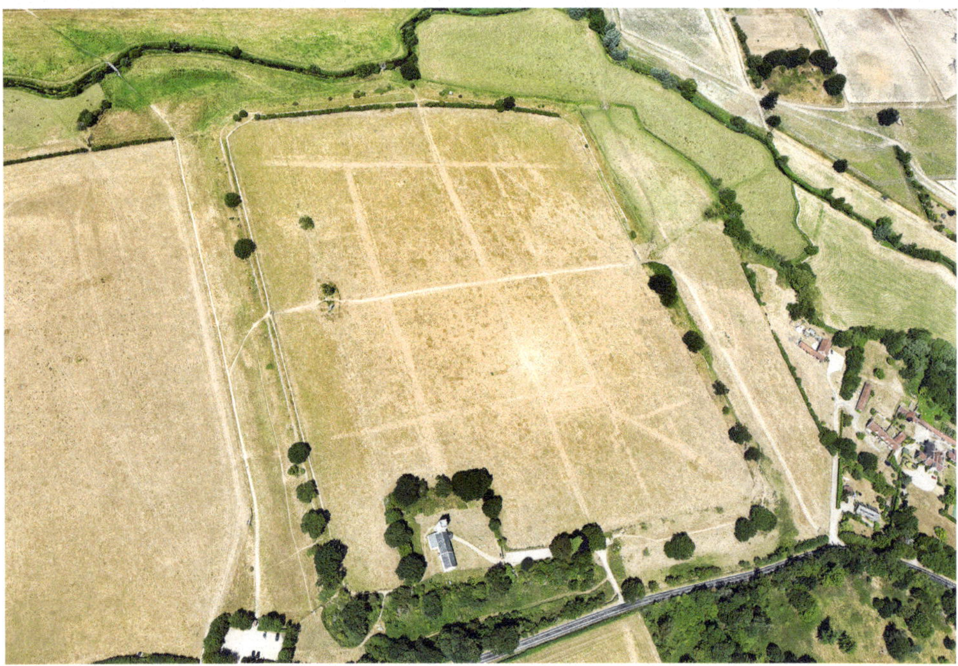

The streets and some of the structures of Venta Icenorum ('the marketplace of the Iceni'), with the Roman regional administrative centre dating from AD 61, at what is now Caister St Edmund were revealed again as crop marks during the dry summer of 2018. (Courtesy of John Fielding)

the rebellion. Roman rule was rapidly re-established and its regional administrative centre of Venta Icenorum (which means 'market place of the Iceni') was formed over the old Iceni settlement at what is now Caistor St Edmund.

Roman rule was further enforced by the construction of roads and the improvement of communications and defences across the eastern counties. The village of Holme-next-the-Sea was the terminus of the Roman road known as the Peddars Way, which traverses Norfolk from Brettenham to its terminus at Holme where there may have been a ferry crossing across the Wash to the Roman road that came down to the sea near Skegness. At nearby Thornham there is an early Roman defensive enclosure that may have contained a beacon or signalling station to communicate with the units of the Tenth Legion across the waters in Lincolnshire. Similar signal stations at Gramborough Hill at Salthouse, Mucklebugh Hill at Kelling and Warborough Hill at Stiffkey are thought to have enabled the Romans to signal along this coastline.

A few miles from Holme at Brancaster was the Roman coastal fort of Branodunum, which was built from imported sandstone in a square shape, enclosing an area of around 2.5 hectares and surrounded by a defensive ditch. Branodunum is believed to have been the most northerly in a chain of around ten forts built in the third century AD along the coast down to Porchester, near modern-day Portsmouth. They acted as bases and fortifications for Roman military units who were patrolling the coastline to protect it from Saxon and Frank raiders.

Two tiles found on the site stamped with the title '1st Cohort of Aquitanians' suggest these men were the first to garrison Brancaster Fort. This fort also provided a shore base for part of the Roman fleet anchored in readiness just off the coast in case raiders

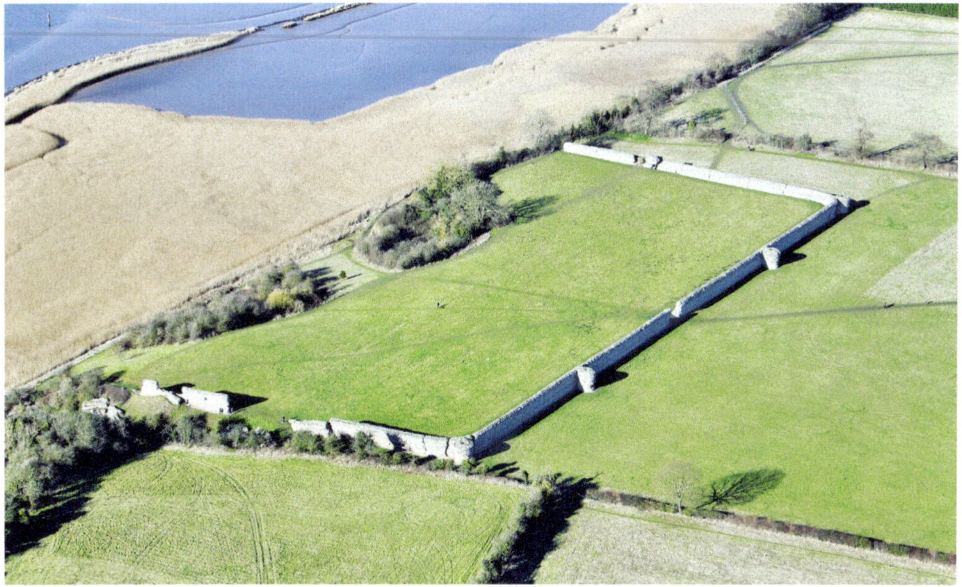

The Roman shore fort at Burgh Castle constructed around the third century AD. (Courtesy of John Fielding)

attempted to enter the Wash. There was probably a shore fort further along the coast on land that once stood beyond Cromer and Mundesley that has long been washed away, so the next fortifications of the Roman period along our coast are found guarding either side of what was a great estuary where the rivers Ant, Bure, Yare and Waveney entered the sea. This area is now mostly dry and is occupied by Great Yarmouth. On the north bank was Caister Fort, built shortly after AD 200 for a garrison of 500–1,000 men of the Roman army and to provide a safe harbour for its naval vessels. Across the estuary to the south was Burgh Castle (probably known as Gariannonum), which was also large enough for 500–1,000 foot soldiers, or up to 500 mounted troops and their horses. Roman cavalry from the Rhineland, the *equites stablesiani*, were based at Burgh in AD 395.

In AD 410 the Emperor Honorius withdrew the last of his military units, leaving the occupants of Roman Norfolk to fend for themselves. Rather than falling as a result of bloody enemy action, many settlements were simply deserted and defences were left to rot and be robbed for building materials over the ensuing years.

Saxons and Vikings

In the years immediately after the withdrawal of the Romans, raiders from Germany, Scandinavia and the Low Countries began Anglo-Saxon colonies in the east and the north of Britain. By the seventh century a number of great Saxon kingdoms had emerged across the country. Norfolk was the northern – 'North Folk' – half of the Kingdom of East Anglia, ruled by the Anglo-Saxon Wuffing dynasty.

England was also subjected to raids in the ninth and tenth centuries, and eventually settlement by Scandinavian Vikings. The vanguard came in the form of a great Viking army led by Ivar the Boneless, who took up winter quarters in Thetford AD 869–870 then began a bloody campaign of conquest and plunder. Edmund, King of East Anglia, attempted to make peace with the Danes but was put to death after battle at Hoxne, Suffolk, in AD 870. Venerated as a saint for his martyrdom, St Edmund became the patron saint of England until he was replaced by St George in the fourteenth century.

The Vikings settled in Norfolk and integrated with a number of local communities. In the emerging county town of Norwich, they constructed defences consisting of an earth bank topped with a wooden fence (demolished by the Normans in the 1100s). So great was the settlement and control of the kingdom of East Anglia that it became known as the Danelaw until East Anglia was taken by Edward the Elder in AD 917 and became part of the Kingdom of England. Vikings raiders came again in 1004 when the Danish King Sweyn Forkbeard raided Thetford and proceeded to Norwich, plundering and burning the town. King Sweyn returned again in 1010, this time burning Thetford.

2. Conquerors and Castles

During the 100 years after the Battle of Hastings (1066) the Norman conquerors displayed their authority and power by constructing Norfolk's first stone castles.

The first Norman regional centre in Norfolk was established in Thetford, at the time one of the largest towns in England. William I appointed Ralph Guader, Earl of East Anglia, control of Thetford. Seeking even loftier office, Guader led an unsuccessful revolt against the Crown in 1075 and was replaced by the king's trusted ally Roger Bigod. Either one of these men could have been responsible for topping off the 80-foot mound with a timber castle, creating the tallest medieval earthwork in Britain. This same process deepened the Iron Age ditches that surrounded it to create an impressive and foreboding fortification. A further castle, known as 'Red Castle', was built on the far side of Thetford when the town's defences were extended during the civil war of King Stephen's reign (1135–54). It had no mound, consisting only of a circular enclosure and defended by a bank and ditch.

Old Buckenham Castle was built by Norman baron and administrator William d'Albini shortly after 1066 as an earth and timber ringwork and bailey fortress. All that remains of this structure today are some remnants of its earthworks and some of the flint stone rubble curtain wall. A new castle was built by the d'Albini family in 1145 that was located 2 miles north-west from the original. It consisted of a circular, flint rubble keep with a circular rampart, an inner bailey, two outer baileys and a wet ditch, and it was besieged during the Barons' War in 1263. The fortification fell to ruin and was finally demolished by its then owner, Sir Philip Knyvet, in 1649. All that is left today are the remains of the circular keep, earth ramparts and the wet ditch.

Castle Acre Castle was founded shortly after 1066 by William de Warenne, 1st Earl of Surrey, who fought beside William the Conqueror at the Battle of Hastings. The castle

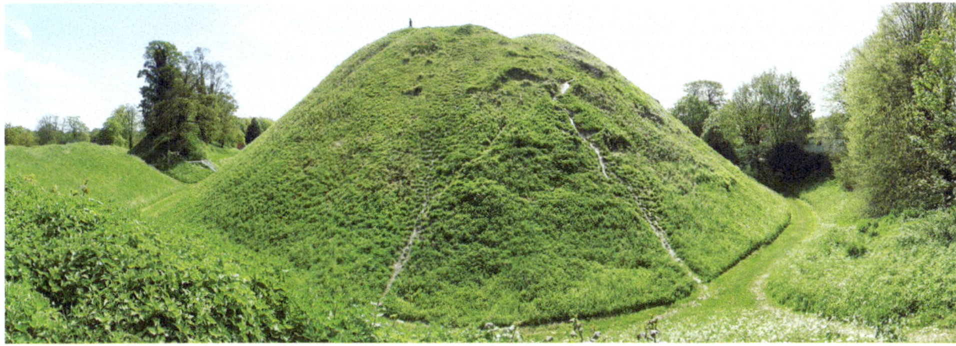

The 80-foot Thetford Castle mound, the tallest medieval earthwork in Britain. For an idea of scale, look for the man standing on the top of the mound.

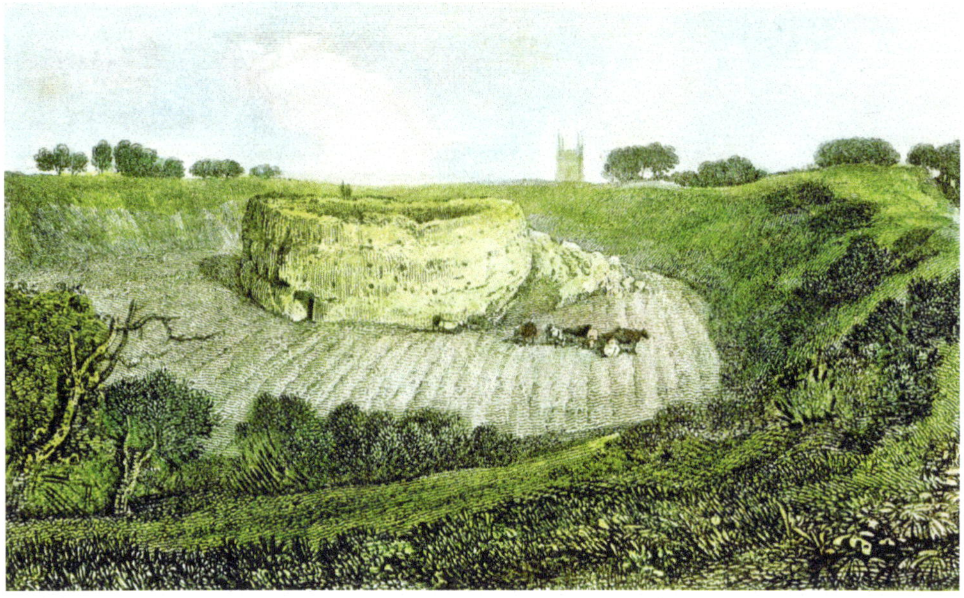

Engraving of New Buckenham Castle, one of John Sell Cotman's illustrations for Thomas Cromwell's *Excursions in the County of Norfolk*, 1818.

was constructed in the centre of de Warenne's estates in Norfolk, near the intersection of the River Nar and the Peddars Way. During the Anarchy (1135–53), as potential heirs and their supporters scrabbled for the Crown of England, the earthworks were raised, the inner and outer baileys were topped with stone walls and the old hall at the centre of the complex was converted into a square keep. By 1397 the castle was in ruins.

Norwich Castle was begun shortly after the Norman Conquest. An area of land was cleared, defensive ditches were dug and a wooden fort was erected atop a great mound. Work was begun on a stone keep in 1094 by William II and was continued after his death by his brother, Henry I. Norwich Castle was completed by 1121. Designed more as a royal residence and a symbol of power rather than a fortification, it has spent the greatest part of its life as the county gaol. It served as such from the fourteenth century until 1883, when the prisoners were removed to the new prison off Plumstead Road and work began on converting the ancient castle into a museum, a purpose it serves to this day.

Castle Rising Castle was built around 1138 by William d'Albini for his new wife, Adeliza of Louvain, the widow of Henry I. It was built more as a home and symbol of power and status than as a fortress. William (son of William d'Albini, the builder of Buckenham Castle) was a staunch supporter of King Stephen and helped arrange a truce between him and Henry Plantagenet that resulted in the Treaty of Wallingford, which brought an end to the Anarchy (1135–53). The castle was sold to Thomas Howard, Duke of Norfolk, in 1544 and still remains in the Howard family to this day. It is one of the best preserved and decorated keeps in England and is surrounded by some of the most impressive earthworks in the country.

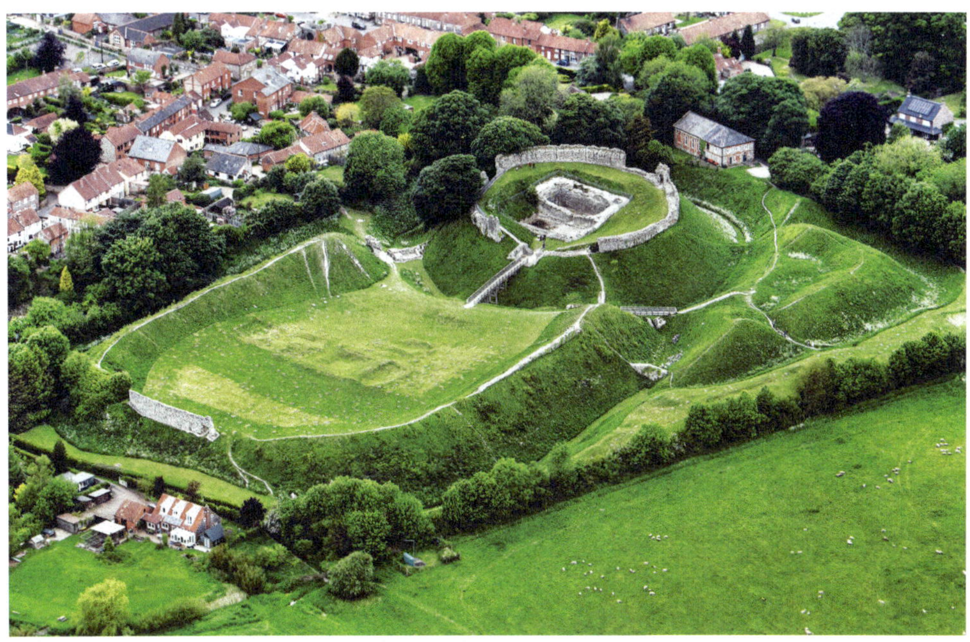

The ruins of Castle Acre Castle, showing the keep, rampart, inner and outer baileys. (Courtesy of John Fielding)

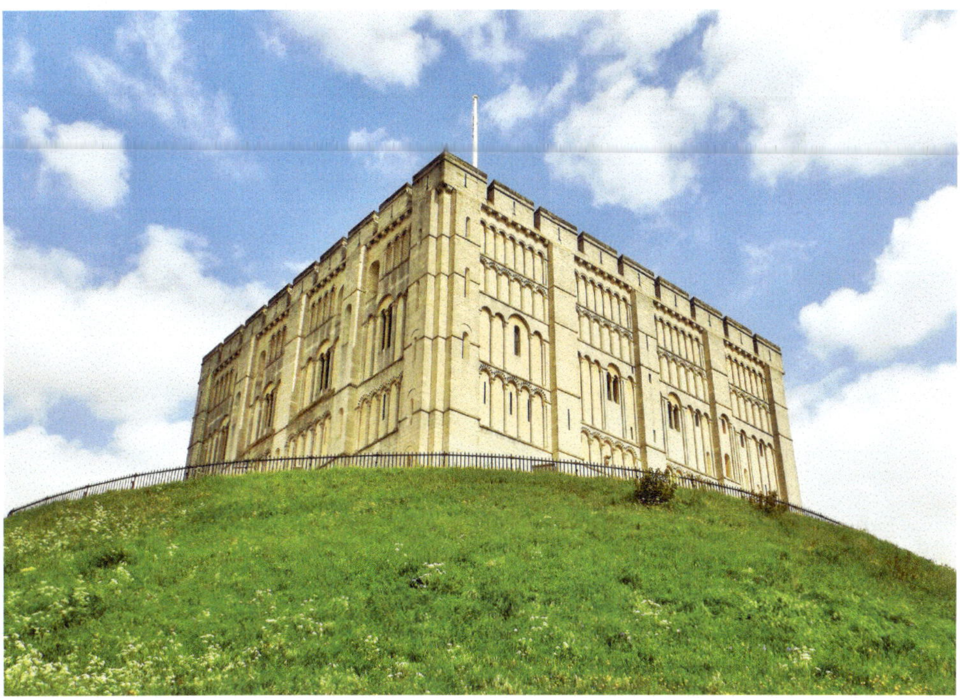

Norwich Castle mound and stone keep. The castle was begun by William Rufus in 1094 and completed in 1121, then refaced in Bath stone in 1834–39.

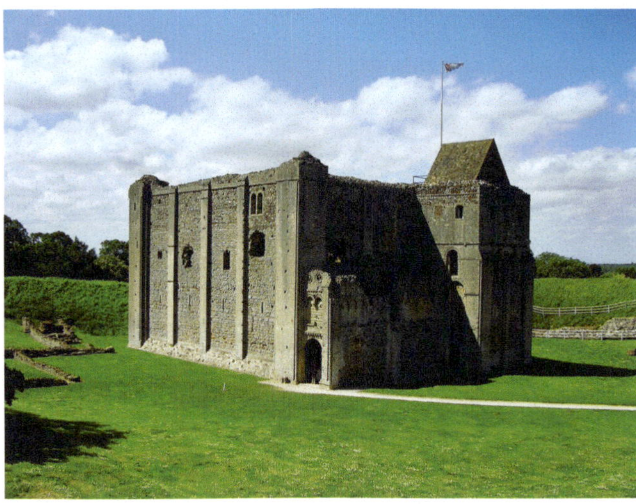

Castle Rising Castle, built more as a symbol of power and status than a fortification, is surrounded by some of the most impressive earthworks in Britain.

Caister Castle was commissioned by Sir John Fastolf in 1432. It is the only example of a Wasserburg castle in the country and one of the first major brick buildings in England. After the death of Fastolf the castle devolved to John Paston. Fastolf's other heirs did not accept Paston's ownership, however, and after years of legal battles they sold what rights they had to John de Mowbray, the Duke of Norfolk. The Wars of the Roses saw battles breaking out around Britain and the duke used the war as a vehicle to lay siege to Caister with 3,000 men in 1469. The garrison of thirty men led by John Paston Jr held out for two months, but after being severely damaged the castle fell to the duke's men. The castle was eventually returned to the Paston family after the death of de Mowbray in 1476.

There are a number of other properties in Norfolk that claim the title 'castle' but these tend to be fortified manor houses, built or fortified after they were granted licences to crenellate (to add parapets, battlements and arrow holes to enable the defence of the property) between the twelfth and fifteenth centuries – such as Weeting Castle (twelfth century), Claxton Castle (fourteenth century) and Baconsthorpe Castle (fifteenth century). The finest example is the moated Oxburgh Hall, which was begun in 1482 by Sir Edmund Bedingfield.

Defensive Walls

The city of Norwich and principle towns of Norfolk all began the construction of flint walls during the thirteeth century. These would not only provide protection from attack but would also regulate who could enter, thereby excluding the likes of undesirables and those carrying contagious diseases. It also meant that market traders could be regulated and inhabitants within the walls could be subject to taxes, including contributions known as 'murage' for the construction and upkeep of the walls and the purchase and maintenance of weaponry.

Yarmouth's walls dates from 1261 when Henry III granted the right to enclose the town with a wall and a ditch. Work began in 1276, but with the labour being provided by citizens working on the wall for a set number of days every year, it took 111 years to complete. Yarmouth's walls stood 23 feet high and were 1.3 miles long punctuated by

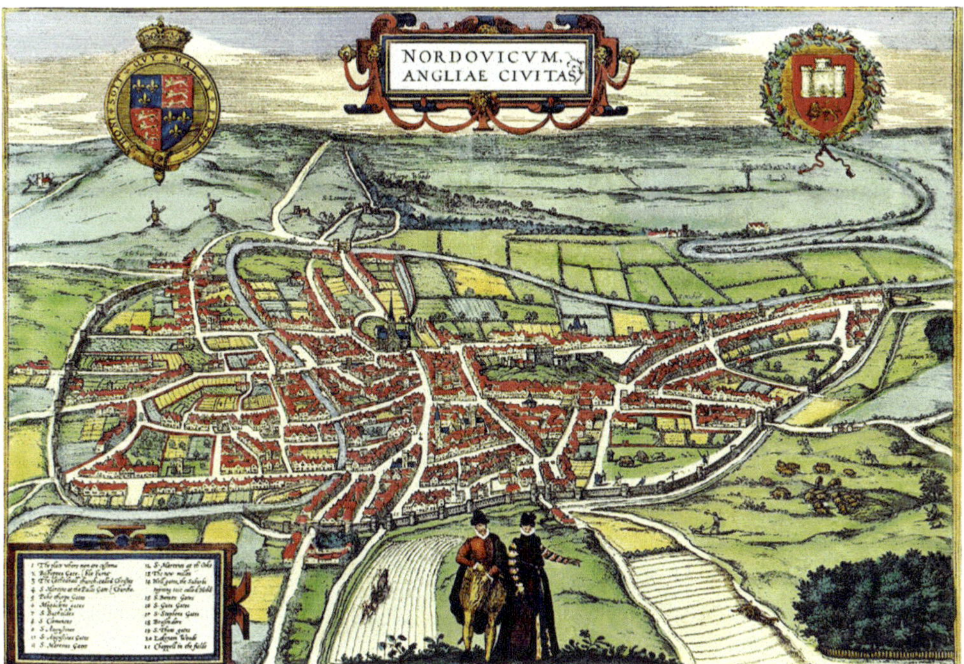

Oblique view map of Norwich seen from the north-west, showing the city wall, published in Braun and Hogenberg's *Civites Orbis Tarrarus*, 1581.

towers and gates, with two principle gates at the north and the south of the town. Some sections of the wall have deteriorated but much still stands. With eleven towers still surviving, Yarmouth can proudly claim to have the second most complete medieval town walls in England – second only to York.

Norwich city walls were started in 1294 and were completed in 1342. Many citizens complained at the cost being levied for the construction of the walls and work came to a standstill on more than one occasion. In the end the walls were completed thanks to the funding of a single wealthy and patriotic individual – Norwich tradesman Richard Spynk. Norwich's city walls were 2.5 miles in length, forming the longest circuit of urban defences in Britain.

King's Lynn also began its defences in the late thirteenth century when the town was surrounded by an earthwork and a ditch. Stone palisades were added later, along with three postern gates and stone gatehouses at the main entrances to the town in the south and east in the fifteenth century. In 1539 Richard Morison enumerated the king's defence programme, noting, 'Lynne shall be made strong.' However, no major works were noted until scares of invasion by the French in 1570 prompted the construction of a small fort known as St Anne's Castle, where the Fisher Fleet joined the Ouse at Lynn's North End.

The defensive walls of Yarmouth, Lynn and Norwich were last put into a state of defence at the time of the English Civil War and were subsequently unmaintained. Ruined sections of the walls, towers and bastions of all three locations can still be seen today.

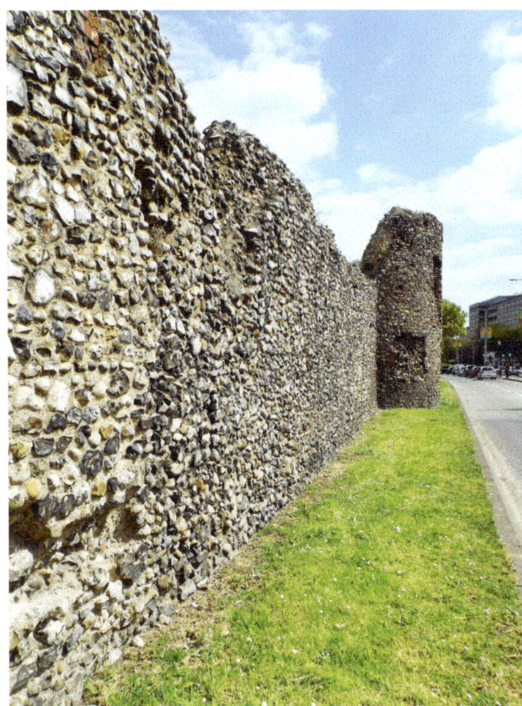

A well-preserved section of Norwich's fourteenth-century defensive wall and one of its bastion towers at Chapel Field.

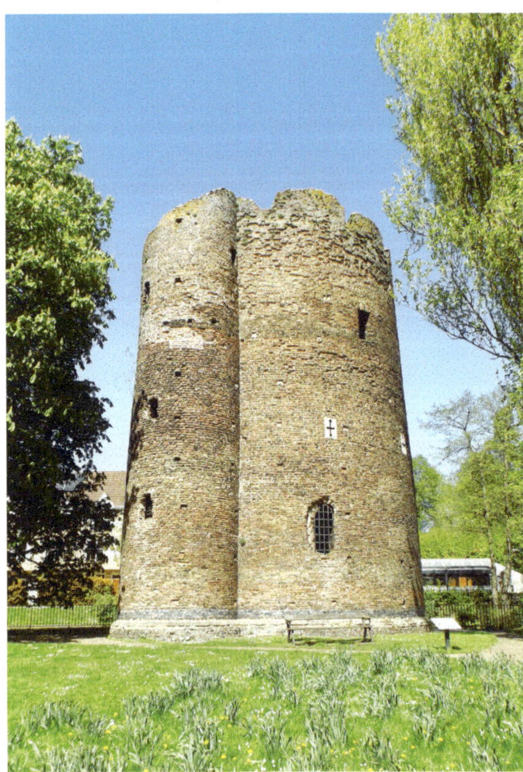

The Cow Tower, Riverside. Built 1398–99 as part of the defences of Norwich, it is one of the earliest purpose-built artillery blockhouses in England.

3. Revolt, Rebellion and the Spanish Armada

Peasants' Revolt, 1381

The unpopular poll tax that had been introduced in 1380 had hit the peasants of England particularly hard, leading them to rise up to protest at a number of places across the country. In June 1381, Geoffrey 'John' Litster (also spelt Litester), a dyer of some means from Felmingham, led a rising in the north-eastern part of the county. Rebels also arrived in Thetford, spreading revolt in the south-west of the county towards the Fens. Rebels converged on Norwich, Lynn and Swaffham. The main force in the county assembled on Mousehold Heath and marched on Norwich, where they caused considerable damage to the property and possessions of poll tax collectors and officials, destroying legal records such as court rolls and taxation documents as they went; a further attack was made on Great Yarmouth.

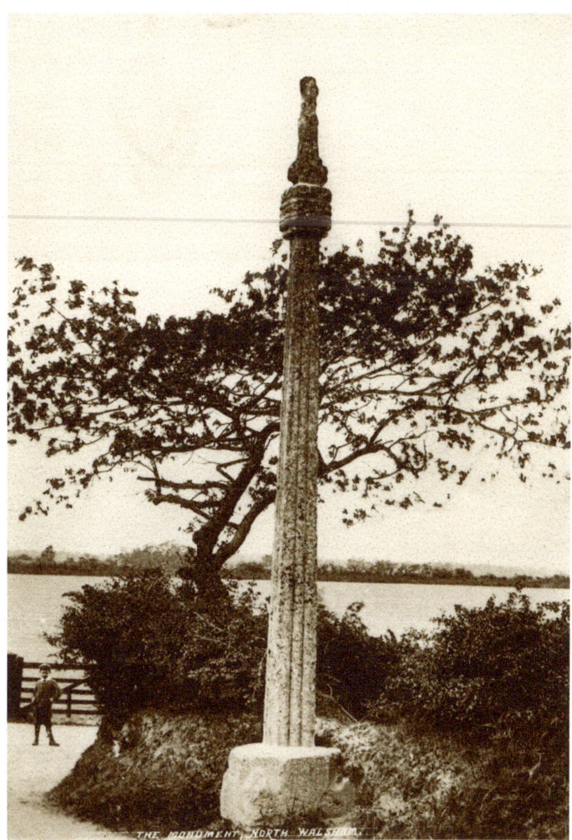

The best preserved of the three remaining monuments to the Battle of North Walsham Heath, which brought a bloody end to the Peasants' Revolt in Norfolk in 1381.

Henry le Despenser, the fighting Bishop of Norwich, set off with his own armoured retinue to intercept the insurgents, gathering support from those who opposed the rebels as he rode across the county. Litster and his rebels fell back to North Walsham Heath where, on 25 or 26 June 1381, a bloody battle ensued. The rebels were no match for Despenser's better trained and equipped men. The denouement of the battle was the slaughter of the peasants who had fled to the unconsecrated footings of the new church in North Walsham after they mistakenly believed they might be able to claim sanctuary there. Litster was captured and hanged, drawn and quartered. His remains were displayed at Norwich, Yarmouth, Lynn and his home near North Walsham as a stern warning to any other who would consider rebellion.

Kett's Rebellion, 1549

On 6 July 1549 the feast of the translation of St Thomas Becket was celebrated at Wymondham. Recent enclosures of land around the town provided the touchpaper for local folk to rise up and start smashing down fences at Hethersett. When the mob arrived at Robert Kett's enclosures he joined them and helped tear down his own fences.

The rioters mustered again in Wymondham on 8 July and marched on Norwich with Robert Kett at their head. Refused entry by the city, the rebel force made camp upon Mousehold, established a council headed by Kett, who sat under the 'Oak of Reformation', and drew up a charter of demands righting the wrongs done to commoners. A royal herald came to Kett's camp and offered a pardon, but Kett refused, saying they had offended

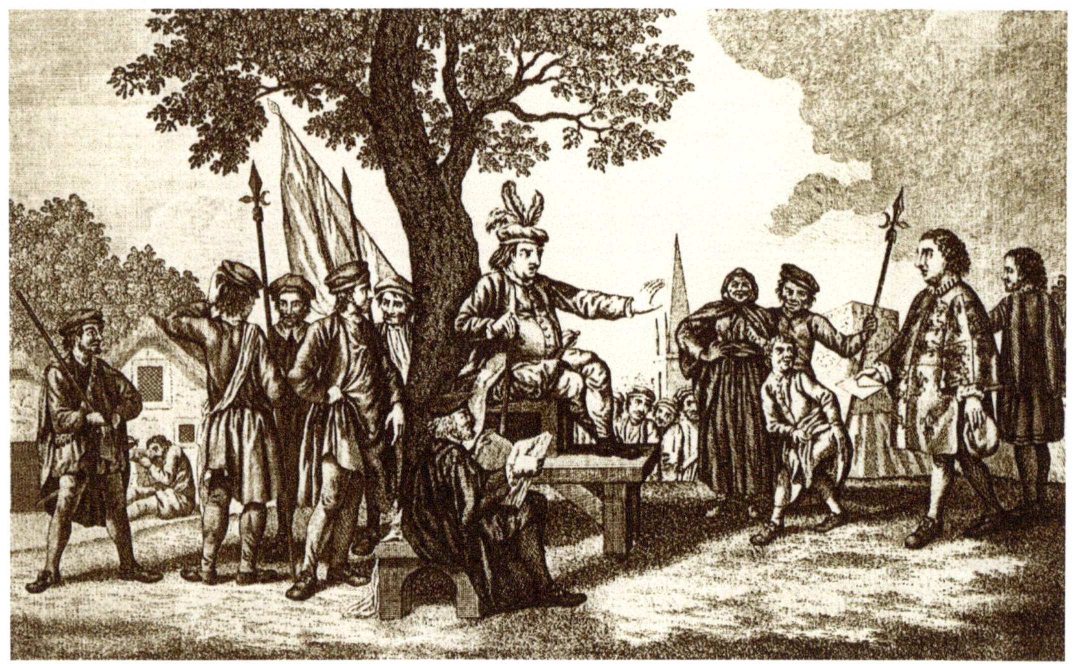

A nineteenth-century impression of Robert Kett, leader of the rebels, sending a King's Herald offering terms away from his 'court' on Mousehold Heath, 1549.

no laws and did not require one; a boy then stepped forward and defecated in front of the herald to show his contempt. The herald went away, denouncing Kett as a traitor. The following day the rebels stormed the city.

A royal army under the Marquess of Northampton arrived at Norwich on 31 July. The rebels fell back but returned again the same night. The fighting continued into the early hours and resulted in many deaths, including that of Lord Sheffield. A considerably larger force – 14,000 men – under the Earl of Warwick arrived at the city on 23 August and another herald offered Kett a pardon, but was again rejected. Three days of intense fighting then commenced, with the final battle fought upon Dussin's Dale. A total of 3,000 rebels were slain. The rebellion was ultimately put down and many of the surviving rebels were publicly hanged as a warning to others. The worst fate, however, awaited the Kett brothers. Robert was paraded through Norwich and brought to the foot of the castle where a rope was then fixed about his neck and he was drawn up to a gibbet upon the battlements and left hanging there until his body wasted away. On the same day his brother William was hanged from the west tower of Wymondham Abbey as warnings to all.

The Spanish Armada

As the threat from Spain became more apparent in 1588 Norfolk was put into a state of defence. Sir Thomas Leighton, commander of Her Majesty's forces in Norfolk, Suffolk and Essex, commissioned a survey of the coast to ascertain the vulnerable points that required fortification. Military engineer Captain York drew up ambitious plans for the defence of Norfolk. He suggested the enlargement of the earth fortification at Weybourne, the construction of a new fort at Cley Haven and a rampart between the two. Further

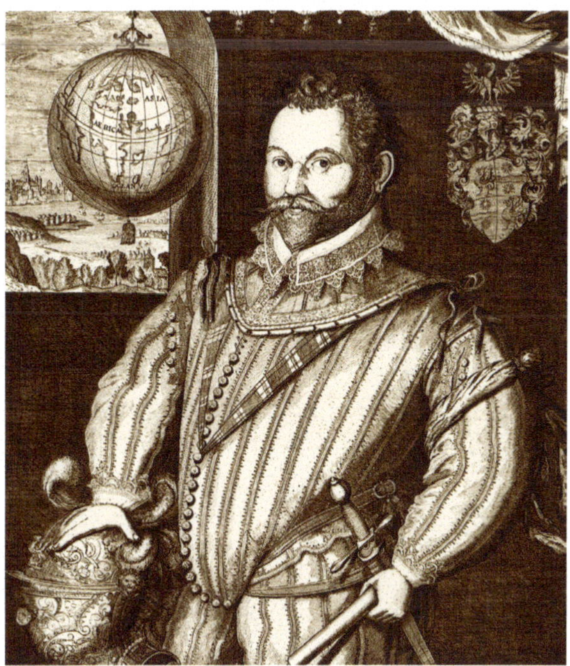

Sir Francis Drake (*c.* 1540–96), vice admiral in command of the English fleet at the time of the Spanish Armada invasion threat of 1588.

defences were planned at Great Yarmouth, Norwich, Acle, Potter Heigham, Wroxham and Wayford Bridge to prevent penetrations by the enemy. A strong bulwark was ordered to be constructed at the Crotch for the protection of Lynn as it commanded a strait, up which ships might sail into the town. Ships could ride close to Sheringham, Mundesley, Bacton and Winterton and land troops, so defences were also ordered for those areas. However, few of these recommendations were actually carried out because the danger from the Armada had passed before considerable works could be undertaken.

In March 1588 three Spanish ships were discovered off Yarmouth taking soundings in diverse places, giving weight to the assumption that an assault on England would begin on the east coast. Sir Francis Drake called upon the burgesses of Yarmouth to contribute to the navy. In April 1588 an agreement was made with Captain William Musgrave to have his ship *The Grace of God* made ready to enter Her Majesty's service, and the twelve barrels of gunpowder, muskets, culverin and ordnance with their carriages he would require for the purpose were supplied from the storehouse of the borough. At Michaelmas 1588 Norwich city chamberlain Robert Goldsmith recorded that £145 had been spent on gunpowder and various sums of black corslets, cuirasses, swords, daggers, pikes, petronels, sword girdles, shovels, soldiers' coats and other accoutrements for equipping and training of the city's trained bands.

In July 1588 the Spanish fleet was spotted off the south-west coast of Britain. A Norwich contingent of 300 men were sent to Great Yarmouth in keels strewn with sedge, and the country waited and watched. On that fateful night England was mobilised by the lighting of a chain of beacons all along the coast and across the country. The Spanish navy was wrecked, not in battle but by storm, and the towns and cities of England greeted this provident victory with joy. In Norwich muskets and guns were discharged, drummers rolled out patriotic tunes under the Market Cross, the city waits played and the bells of St Peter Mancroft rang out.

4. The English Civil War

The English Civil War (1642–51) saw many communities fractured and bloody battles fought around the country as it was divided between those who supported the king and those who supported Parliament.

Norwich readdressed its defences, reinstating the massive boom chain across the river and the twelve city gates were reduced to nine after those at St Augustine's, Conesford and the Bishop's Gate were locked, barred and stopped up with rubble. A plan to create further defensive bulwarks along the wall and a breastwork along the river from the Boom Towers to Cow Tower were also drawn up. Yarmouth declared for Parliament in July 1642 and the town was put into a state of defence. A town gunner was appointed, a night watch armed with muskets was set at each gate, trained bands were raised and the armed inhabitants of the town primed to be ready to assemble at the sounding of drums. The houses and workshops outside the walls were taken down, the gates rampired and locked and the east leaf of the bridge drawn up every night. At Lynn the old town walls were reinforced, drawbridges renewed, earthworks extended to the north of the Fisher Fleet and the Red Mount Chapel became a gunpowder store.

Norfolk predominantly came out in support for Parliament and the Eastern Association of Parliamentarian militias of Essex, Hertfordshire, Norfolk, Suffolk and Cambridgeshire

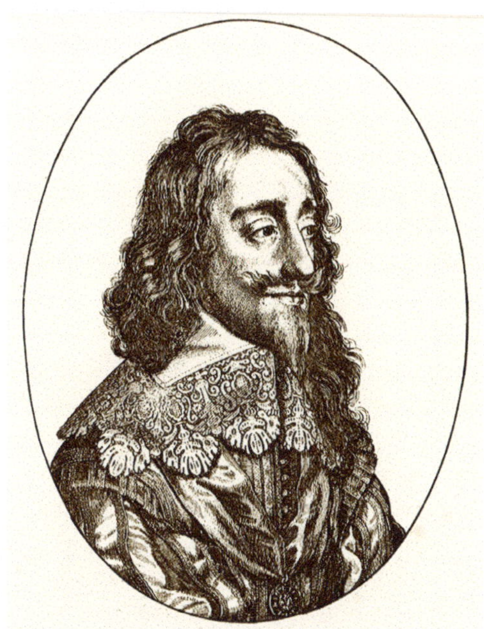

Charles I (1600–49).

was established in December 1642 (the association was later joined by the militias of Huntingdonshire and Lincolnshire). The first commander of the association was General William Grey, and one of the first units to join had been a troop of horse raised by Captain Oliver Cromwell. Over the winter of 1642–43 the Eastern Association established Parliamentary control over East Anglia.

Much of 1643 saw the forces of the Eastern Association fighting northern Royalists as they attempted to secure Lincolnshire for Parliament. In August 1643 Lord Grey was replaced as commander of the Eastern Association by the Earl of Manchester, and Cromwell was made Lieutenant General of Horse. Training also became more frequent and rigorous under the new commanders. The Yarmouth-trained bands, under the command of Sir John Wentworth of Somerleyton, were ordered to assemble once a week at 8 am at the house of William Killett at Gorleston with their arms, powder, match and bullets, ready to drill.

Lynn had shakily declared for Parliament, but Sir Hamon le Strange, a member of the highest echelon of local gentry and a man known for his Royalist sympathies, was appointed governor. He struck a deal with Charles I, whereby if Lynn declared for the Crown the king would send troops. On 28 August 1643 the town closed its doors to a force of some 18,000 Parliamentarian soldiers under the command of the Earl of Manchester. With 500 barrels of gunpowder in store and around forty guns mounted on the ramparts, the town was prepared for a siege. The ensuing six weeks of bombardment caused terrible damage to the defences and dwellings in the town, even St Margaret's Church was blasted during a sermon – a 16-lb shot smashed through a widow, showering parishioners with stained glass and shattering a pillar.

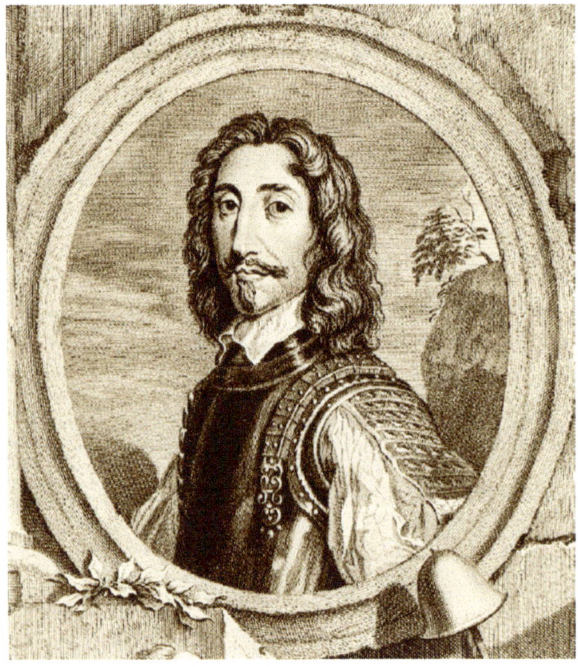

Major-General Edward Montagu, 2nd Earl of Manchester (1602–1671), commander of the Eastern Association of the Army of Parliament.

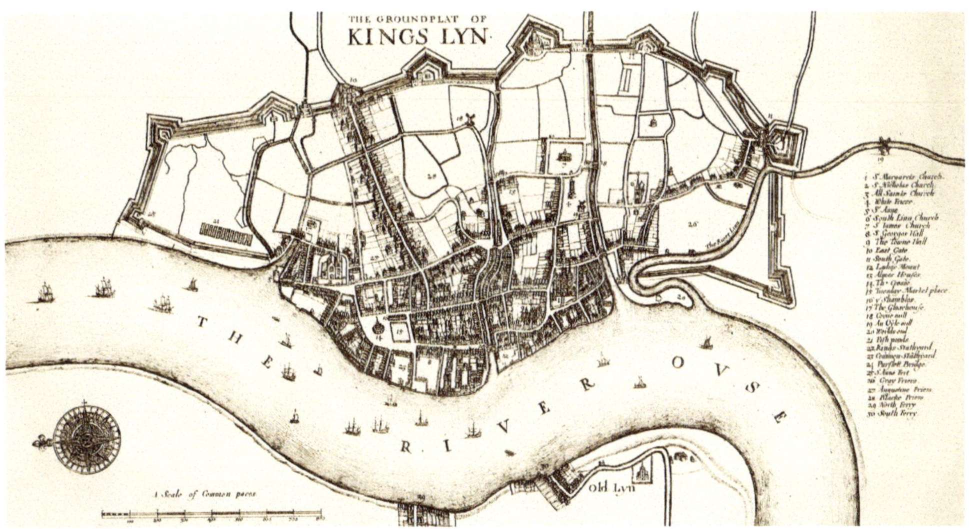

Map of King's Lynn showing its defensive walls and fortifications by Wenceslas Hollar (1607–77).

The casualties incurred during the siege of Lynn were minimal, with figures of up to eighty fatalities being quoted. The Royalist forces within the walls of Lynn were, however, never relieved because the Earl of Warwick blockaded the Wash with his squadron of warships. Growing weak through lack of food, and with no hope of relief, the garrison were finally forced to ask for terms after the besiegers paraded in full strength before the walls of the town. Lynn opened its gates on 16 September 1642 and the Earl of Manchester's army marched in to occupy for Parliament. Once Lynn was secured, Captain Valentine Wauden was appointed governor and the town's defences were renewed with a bastioned enceinte of the latest design. Such were these improvements that King's Lynn became one of the strongest fortresses in East Anglia.

There would be no more sieges and certainly no further battles fought in Norfolk during the Civil War, but that does not mean that there was no more disquiet. In September 1643 an angry Puritan mob sacked Norwich Cathedral – smashing statues, monuments and windows. They also took away vestments, holy objects, service and singing books and burned them in the marketplace. Shots were fired inside the building too. Bishop Joseph Hall stated in his tract *Hard Measure*, 'The cathedral was filled with musketeers, drinking and tobaccoing as freely as if it had turned into an ale house.' The cathedral was abandoned the following year and Cromwell used it for a while as a stable for his cavalry.

There were still rumblings of support for the king among the people of the county. The Prince of Wales, later Charles II, planned to seize Yarmouth in 1648. The town, however, was not willing to co-operate and the attempt was abandoned.

The Great Blowe

Local people did not like the imposition of Puritan values that inflicted unwelcome regulation on places of entertainment, festivals and holidays. Mayor of Norwich John Utting had supported the old traditions, but after complaints were lodged by local

A true

RELATION

OF

The late great Mutiny which was in the
City and County of NORWICH, April 24. 1648.
WITH

That accident that befell those Mutiniers that day:
there being as is thought, above 200. slaine by the fireing of 98.
Barrels of Powder; being truly related in a Letter from th~
City of *Norwich*, to an honourable Person of the honourable House of Commons, with the Votes of
the House concerning the same, and ordered
to be printed, to prevent misinformation.

In foveam quam foderunt &c.

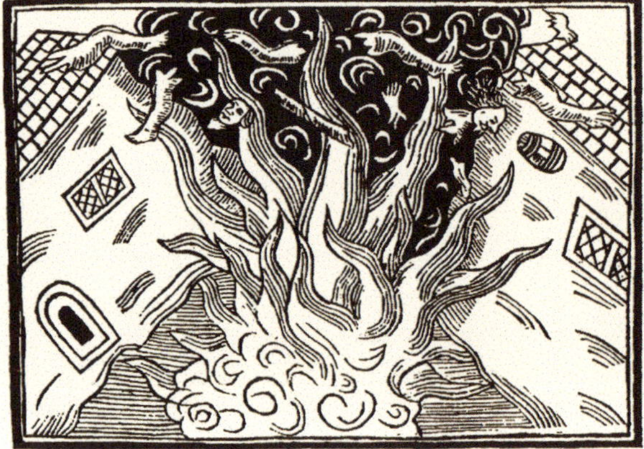

A contemporary account of the
'The Great Blowe', the largest
explosion of the English Civil War.

Puritans an attempt was made by a Parliamentary representative to arrest Utting. When this became known, anger erupted into riot on 24 April 1648. The houses of prominent Norwich Puritans were attacked and a mob stormed the headquarters of the County Committee, not far from St Peter Mancroft Church on what is now known as Bethel Street. A small contingent of Parliamentarian cavalry arrived to put down the rising and running battles broke out as they made their way down St Stephen's Street. More arms were looted from the Committee House, but in their haste to break open some gunpowder casks and carry off the contents, including large quantities of gunpowder carried in their hats, rioters had spilt considerable amounts of it through the building, which ignited and exploded some ninety barrels of gunpowder. To give an idea of the scale of this blast, Guy Fawkes and his conspirators planned to use thirty-six barrels of gunpowder to blow up the Houses of Parliament. What became known as 'The Great Blowe' is believed to have been the largest explosion during the English Civil War: forty rioters were killed and over 120 were injured by the blast, which devastated the immediate vicinity of the explosion. It blew out the windows of St Peter Mancroft and St Stephen's churches and sent timbers, tiles, wood, plaster, stone and lead debris and bits of victims showering down over a large area of the city, bringing the last spasm of the Civil War in Norfolk to a very abrupt end.

5. Revolutionary and Napoleonic Wars

Norfolk has always had a fine reputation for its volunteer soldiery. In the mid-eighteenth century a plan for raising county militias was first proposed. The measure proved so unpopular there were instances of riots around the country, but in Norfolk the men presented themselves with alacrity under the Militia Act of 1757. Two regiments of militia were embodied in the county the following year: the 1st Battalion or West Norfolk and the 2nd Battalion or East Norfolk. Both battalions drew all manner of gentry to both their officer corps and other ranks

In 1759, the East Norfolk was the first regiment of militia to leave its own county, marching under the command of the Earl of Orford to Kensington where it was reviewed by George II, who was greatly pleased by what he saw and raised his hat to every officer. The Prince of Wales (later George III) fell in with them at Richmond and presented each division with a bank note for £50. The Norfolk Militia also had the distinction of being the first unit to have a fully illustrated drill and manoeuvres manual, entitled *A Plan for the Discipline for the use of the Norfolk Militia* – written by William Windham and Colonel George Townshend, 1st Marquess of Townshend (1760).

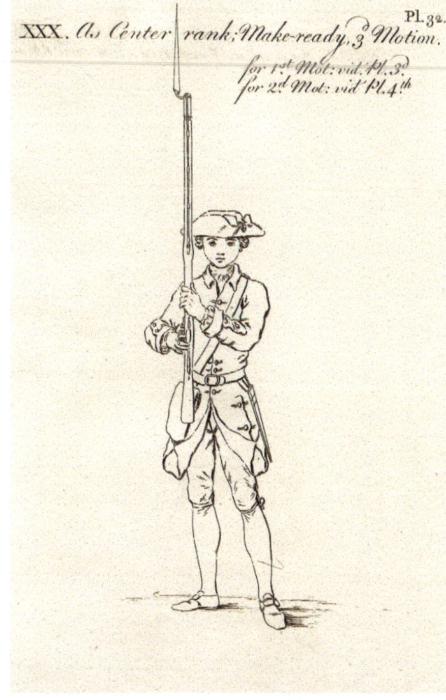

One of numerous plates illustrating drill manoeuvres with musket from *A Plan for the Discipline for the use of the Norfolk Militia,* by William Windham and Colonel George Townshend, 1st Marquess of Townshend (1760), one of the first illustrated, printed training manuals.

Regiments passing through the county recruited Norfolk men and over the next decade or so military life was quiet, but as time passed there were rumblings of revolution in our colonies, culminating in the outbreak of the American War of Independence in 1775. Soon there were actions at sea, and when France and Spain came out in support of America fear of attacks from the sea saw King's Lynn and Great Yarmouth raise and arm town guards and assess their defences. St Anne's Fort at King's Lynn was refitted with ten 18-pounder guns from London and 171 volunteer artillerymen were enrolled to man them. Great Yarmouth did similar, rearming the town fort with eight 24 pounders and four 6 pounders, along with a new earthwork battery with five 32 pounders and ten 24 pounders. A stockaded battery with six 24 pounders at Gorleston on either side of the river mouth and a further three batteries were constructed on the Denes.

Before the days of a formal police force in Britain civil unrest was often quelled by the deployment of mounted troops, so when concerns were raised by the British gentry in the late 1780s that England may rise in revolution as France had, it is not surprising that Norfolk's first purpose-built barracks were to be constructed for the accommodation of regular cavalry. The Norwich Cavalry Barracks were built by the government between the years 1791 and 1793 on the old manor house grounds of Hassett's Hall in Pockthorpe at a cost of around £20,000. Built in red brick, the complex consisted of a central building facing south, with large wings on the east and west forming three sides of a square and containing commodious lodging rooms and stables for three troops of cavalry. The whole thing covered a 10-acre site and was enclosed with a high brick wall.

Over the years 1794–95, committees were set up to raise private subscriptions for the uniforms and equipment of local volunteer units, such as the Lynn Volunteers. Troops of mounted volunteers were also raised, many of whom were farmers riding their own horses – hence they became known as 'yeomanry'. Lord Townshend, alluding to the revolutionary principles then being propagated said, 'They may not do much in case of invasion but they will prevent a great deal.' This was no exaggeration either. Sir James McGrigor stated in his *Autobiography* that his regiment (the 88th Foot), the 53rd Foot and 2nd Dragoon Guards were sent to Norwich 'on account of the turbulent state of the population'. He goes on to explain, 'the revolutionary feeling had found its way from France to England and in no place was the admiration of what had been affected in

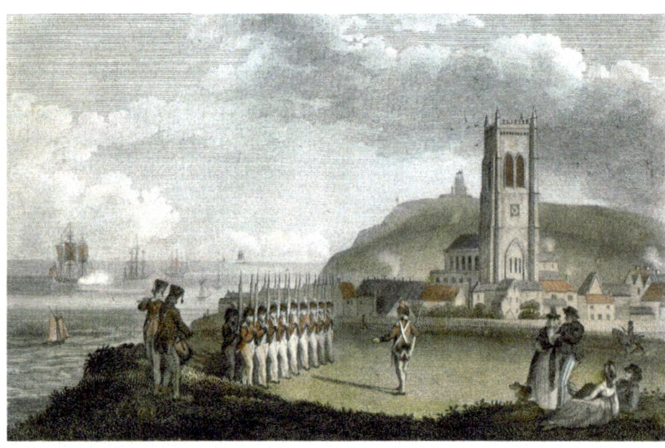

Volunteer militia drill on the Marrams, Cromer, 1798.

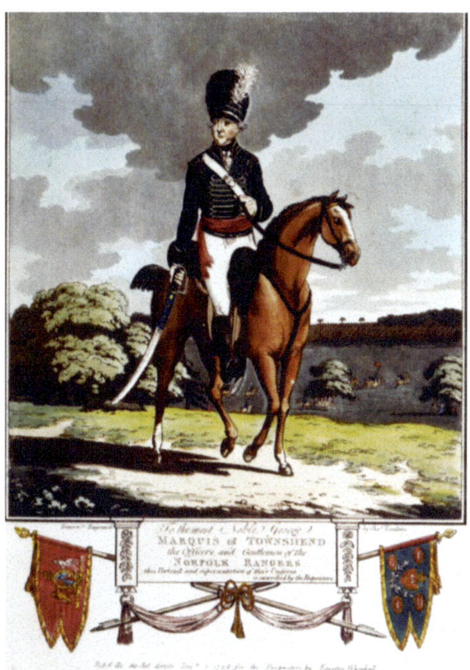

George, Marquess of Townshend, in the uniform
of the Norfolk Rangers, 1799.

France, together with the spirit or republicanism, greater than in Norwich. On our first arrival the officers could hardly appear in the streets without insult from the populace.'

Some £6,000 was subscribed in Norwich for raising a regiment of volunteer infantry, in which 1,400 citizens speedily enrolled themselves. The Norwich Light Horse Volunteers and Norwich Loyal Military Association were embodied in February 1797, the former raised by Robert Harvey and the latter by John Patteson.

There were no permanent barracks for infantry in Norwich, but a facility for returned wounded from the Battle of Camperdown was established in St George's Colegate in 1797 and two large buildings in Coslany Street were converted into temporary barracks. Communicating any danger of invasion was initially left to a system of raising flags in daylight or lighting beacons at dusk and through the hours of darkness. In September 1797 a new telegraph was erected on the top of Norwich Castle to communicate with Strumpshaw Mill, Filby Church and Yarmouth. The following month Norfolk and Norwich volunteer regiments agreed to perform permanent duty at Great Yarmouth in case of invasion, many of whom were stationed in the port during the succeeding two months.

Great Yarmouth raised two separate corps of volunteers in 1798 for the defence of the town: the Yarmouth Regiment of Volunteer Infantry, raised by Captain Joseph Barker Bell; and the Loyal Apollonian Volunteers, with Samuel Paget appointed captain commandant. The latter supplied their own uniforms and covered all expenses with the exception of arms and accoutrements. They engaged to be trained and exercised at least once a week and for no less than three hours at a time. Two further units of volunteers were also raised in the town the same year, the Yarmouth Gentlemen and Yeomanry and the Norfolk Militia Artillery. A further company of 120 Sea Fencibles was also raised.

In 1801 the Lord Lieutenant of Norfolk received a directive to plan measures for the preservation of property in the event of invasion. Deputy Lieutenants and Justices of the Peace were directed to use all means in their power to make sure livestock was removed inland from the coast. Guides were to be procured and pioneers, carriages, bread and supplies in general arranged and returns of people, stock, boats and barges in each area were to be made. General Loftus, the general commanding in Norfolk, prepared a scheme for dividing the maritime hundreds into six divisions, appointing particular Volunteer Corps to each division, nominating places for temporary depots and routes for driving cattle under the protection of the yeomanry to the interior of the county. The volunteers were also advised to exercise frequently and be ready for service at short notice.

On the international stage, Norfolk-born Royal Navy hero Vice Admiral Horatio Nelson had fought a naval campaign across the Mediterranean. Nelson lost his right arm when fighting at Santa Cruz in Tenerife in July 1797. He received a musket ball shot just above his right elbow and the ship's surgeon had no option but to amputate the forearm. Despite his injury he carried on, and it was his tactical genius that was key to the decisive victory of the British fleet at the Battle of the Nile (Aboukir Bay) in Egypt on 1 August 1798. During the battle Nelson was hit above his right eye by a fragment of shot. Bleeding profusely, pale and concussed, he carried on. Nelson did not lose the eye but lost his sight in it and suffered from sporadic blinding headaches caused by this injury for the rest of his life.

Probably the greatest single tragedy in Norfolk during the Napoleonic Wars occurred off Happisburgh with the sinking of HMS *Invincible*, a third-rate, seventy-four-gun ship on 16 March 1801. A strong tide and keen wind sent *Invincible* off course and she struck Hammond's Knoll sandbank, just east of Haisbro Sand. An orderly evacuation was organised for senior officers and the youngest crewmen; the main body of the crew awaited evacuation at dawn, but *Invincible* sank at first light with the loss of 400 hands. A total of 119 members of the ship's company were buried in Happisburgh Churchyard and a fine memorial stone was erected to their memory in 1998.

When war with France renewed in 1803 fears of invasion led to local volunteer forces being raised again. Tar barrel warning beacons were placed on top of church towers and some of the principal residences in the county to create a chain of communication – day or night – in the event of enemy landings. Bonfires were also prohibited at this time lest they cause a false alarm.

The first parade of the Norwich Regiment of Volunteer Infantry took place on 1 September 1803. The new unit consisted of eight battalion companies, a light infantry and grenadier company under Lieutenant Colonel Robert Patteson, and Major Richard Bacon raised a company of riflemen. In December 1803 there were twenty-two units of Yeomanry Cavalry raised in the county, which were formed into three regiments. The Marquess of Townshend was appointed colonel of the Western Regiment; Major-General John Money, the colonel of the Eastern Regiment; and Colonel William Bulwer was made colonel of the Mid-Norfolk Regiment. On 18 January 1804 the Norwich Regiment took the oath of allegiance and received their colours, presented by the mayor in an impressive ceremony in the Market Place.

Norfolk's defences were surveyed again and strengthened in 1804. In addition to the fire beacons, flag staffs were placed at Rainham Hall, Holkham Hall and Houghton Hall.

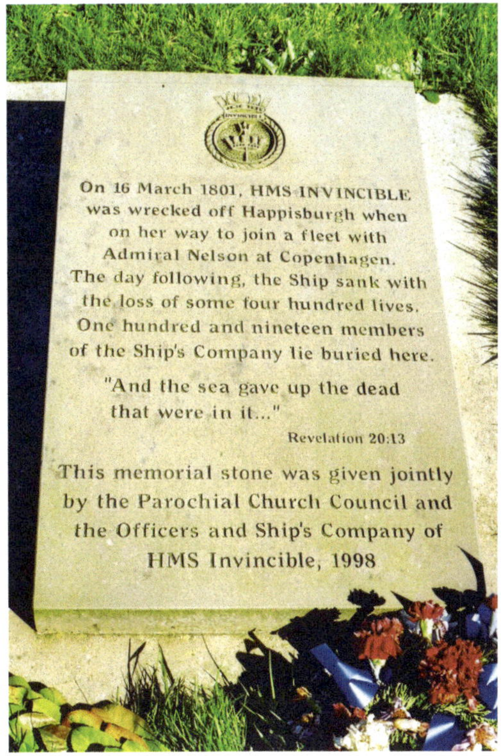

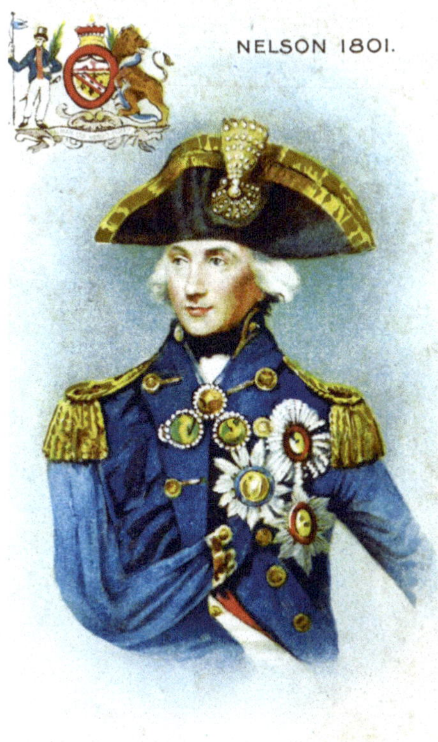

Above left: Memorial stone to the crew that perished when HMS *Invincible* sank off Happisburgh in 1801 with the loss of 400 lives. A total of 119 members of the ship's company were buried in St Mary's Churchyard.

Above right: Vice Admiral Horatio Nelson, 1st Viscount Nelson (1758–1805), our nation's greatest maritime hero and a son of Norfolk.

The red flag was only to be hoisted in case of actual invasion or on the appearance of an enemy on the coast. Weaponry was also checked and in some cases updated, and volunteers' drill and manoeuvres became more rigorous. James Kerr of Great Yarmouth composed a poem to the Volunteers that concludes:

> And should that tyrant stain'd with blood,
> Who helpless nations over-runs; By whom are rul'd with iron rod,
> Batavia's and Helvetia's sons,
> Dare to fulfil his idle boast,
> To bring his band of ruffians here;
> One every point of Albion's coast
> He'll meet – a British Volunteer.

One of the 'sharpest presses' in Great Yarmouth occurred on 9 May 1805, when no fewer than 300 men were impressed. Many were subsequently returned following complaint, but fifty ultimately went on to serve in the Royal Navy. A number of Norfolk men were also present at the Battle of Trafalgar on 1 October 1805, where Nelson defeated the combined navies of France and Spain. It was also the battle in which he received a fatal wound; he died shortly after he learned of victory. Trafalgar had been a triumph, but the war rumbled on.

Yarmouth began to grow in importance as a naval base. In 1806 an armoury for some 10,000 stand of arms was erected with suitable stores capable of equipping two ships of the line, four frigates and six sloops. During the late summer of 1807 an impressive British fleet assembled in the Yarmouth Roads under the command of Admiral James Gambier and set sail for the Baltic. It would prove to be the last time a true wooden 'hearts of oak' fleet sailed into action from Yarmouth. Around six weeks after their departure the fleet was engaged at the Second Battle of Copenhagen. They were victorious and sent around sixty-four captured vessels back to the Yarmouth Roads.

In 1808 a chain of Admiralty shutter telegraphs were established between the naval ports of Chatham, Deal, Portsmouth, Plymouth and Great Yarmouth and the Admiralty in London. Each signal station was built around 7 to 10 miles apart from each other, and in Norfolk ran from the top of one of the towers of the South Gate at Yarmouth on to Strumpshaw, Thorpe Hills, Wreningham, Carlton Rode, East Harling, Thetford, over Newmarket Heath, across Cambridgeshire and on to London. In total there were eighteen signal stations to cover the 146 miles between Yarmouth and the Admiralty. The system was extremely efficient and meant that messages that could take a day or more to send by river, sea or road could be sent between the Admiralty office in Whitehall and Yarmouth in around seventeen minutes.

From 1807 the volunteers slowly faded away as the danger of invasion passed and their government funding was slashed. Those remaining were transferred to local militia battalions. The Volunteer Corps of Norwich and Norfolk were finally disbanded 24 March 1813 and their arms were returned to store after Napoleon's defeat at the Battle of Waterloo in 1815. Norfolk links with the battle lingered on, however, as some 600 of the wounded from Waterloo were lodged at the Royal Naval Hospital that had opened in 1809 on the South Denes at Great Yarmouth.

6. The Victorian and Edwardian Eras

The reigns of Queen Victoria (1837–1901) and Edward VII (1901–10) are marked by colonial wars fought all over the world that expanded the British Empire, but Britain itself experienced a long period of peace without major internal strife. Up until the 1870s the Norwich Cavalry Barracks remained the only permanent facility for regular troops in Norfolk and a host of cavalry units, including Dragoons, Hussars and Lancers, were stationed there as they toured the cavalry stations of England for spells of duty of around twelve months in each station.

The Crimean War (1853–56) prompted the army to consider the mobilisation of the militia. The old armoury buildings in Southtown, Great Yarmouth, that had been sold off after the end of the Napoleonic Wars were taken over by the army again and converted into militia barracks in 1855 for the staff of the East Norfolk Militia and the Norfolk Artillery Militia. Furthermore, the machinations of France in the 1850s led the Secretary of War to issue a circular to lord lieutenants in 1859 authorising them to accept the services of companies of volunteers.

At a meeting of citizens held in the Norwich's Guildhall on 23 May 1859 it was resolved to raise a Norwich Rifle Corps. By 5 July the first three companies had been formed and a headquarters established in the old militia barracks in the city at St Catherine's Close. The 1st Norfolk Artillery Volunteer Corps was formed at Great Yarmouth on 29 September 1859, with further batteries in Yarmouth and Norwich raised in 1860–63.

Despite the fears coming to nothing, volunteer defence forces were retained and within five years a network of volunteer infantry, rifles and artillery had been established across England and Wales.

The first purpose-built volunteer drill hall in Norwich, the Chapel Field Drill Hall, was opened with due ceremony by the Prince and Princess of Wales on their first visit to Norwich on 30 October 1866. The following year (1867) the Drill Hall for Rifle Volunteers in Great Yarmouth was built on St Peter's Plain.

The Cardwell Reforms 1868–74 modernised both the British Army's structure and its equipment. Among the changes was the creation of a system of recruiting areas based on counties, instituted in 1873. Norfolk was designated the 9th Regimental District with the old militia barracks on Southtown Road, Great Yarmouth, becoming the depot for the two battalions of the 9th (East Norfolk) Regiment of Foot. Although the 9th Regiment had recruited in the county for many years before and had freely adopted the 'East Norfolk' appellation to the name of the regiment, this was their first depot in the county.

The Childers Reforms of 1881 reorganised the infantry regiments of the British Army from numbered regiments of foot to county regiments. The old 9th (East Norfolk) Regiment became the Norfolk Regiment. Every regiment was to be organised along

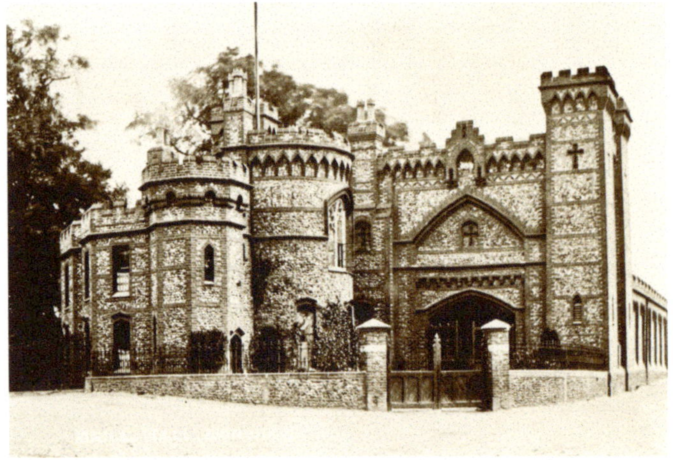

The Chapel Field Drill Hall, the first purpose-built Volunteer Drill Hall in Norwich, photographed in the early twentieth century.

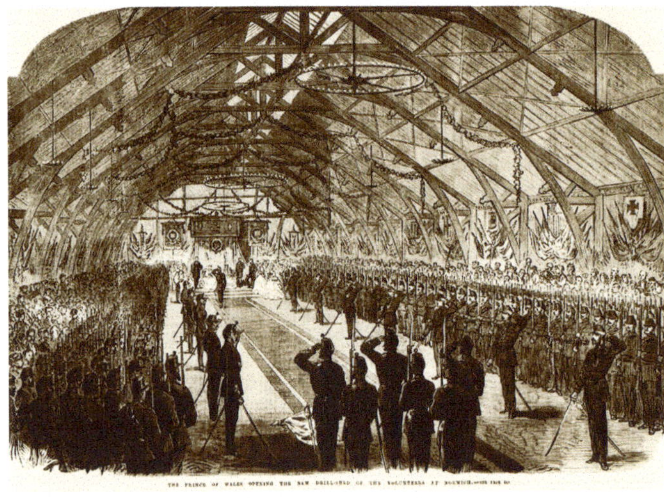

The opening of the Chapel Field Drill Hall by the Prince and Princess of Wales on 30 October 1866.

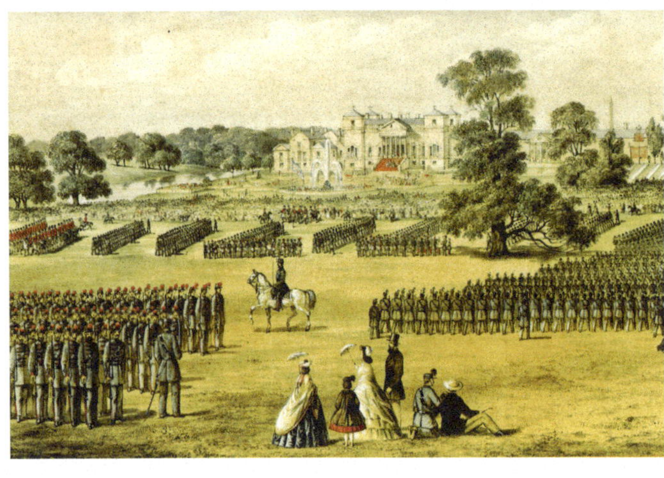

Grand Review of Norfolk Volunteers, Holkham, 21 September 1861.

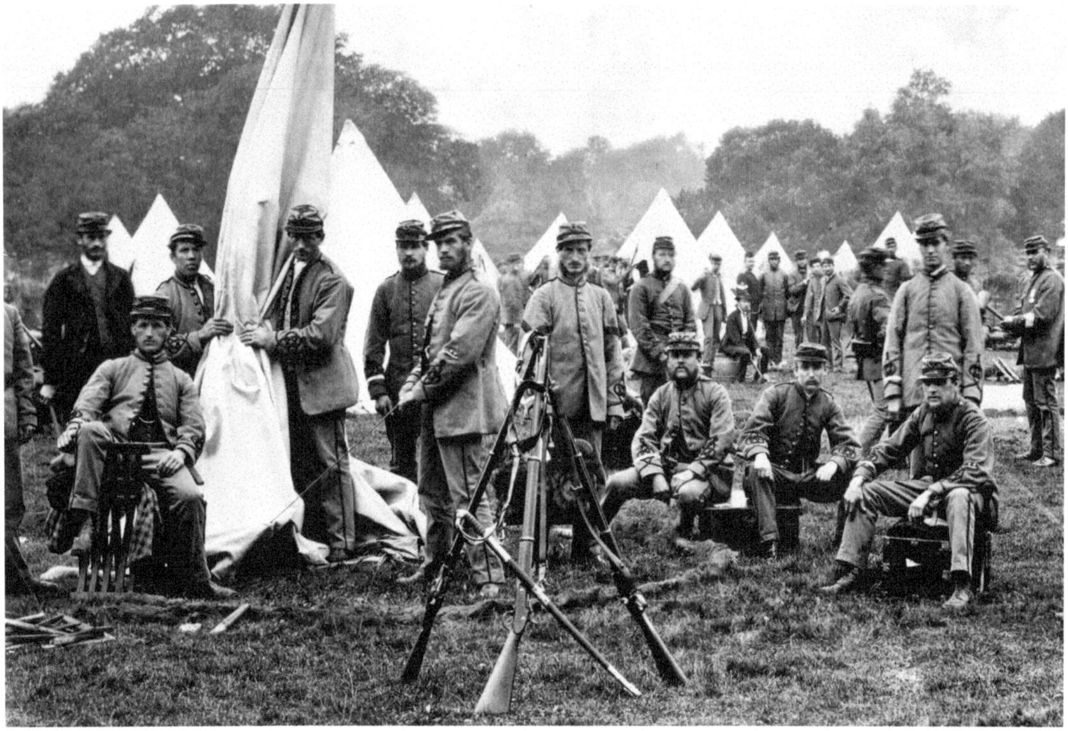

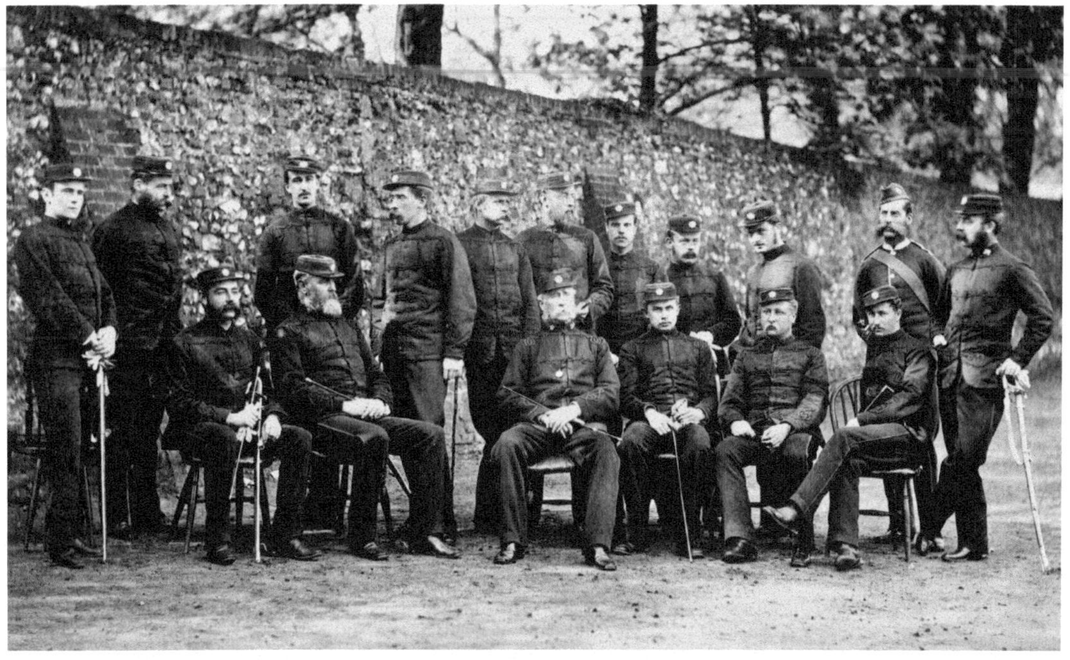

Members of the Norfolk Rifle Volunteers striking camp 1872.

Officers of the City of Norwich Rifle Volunteers, 1872.

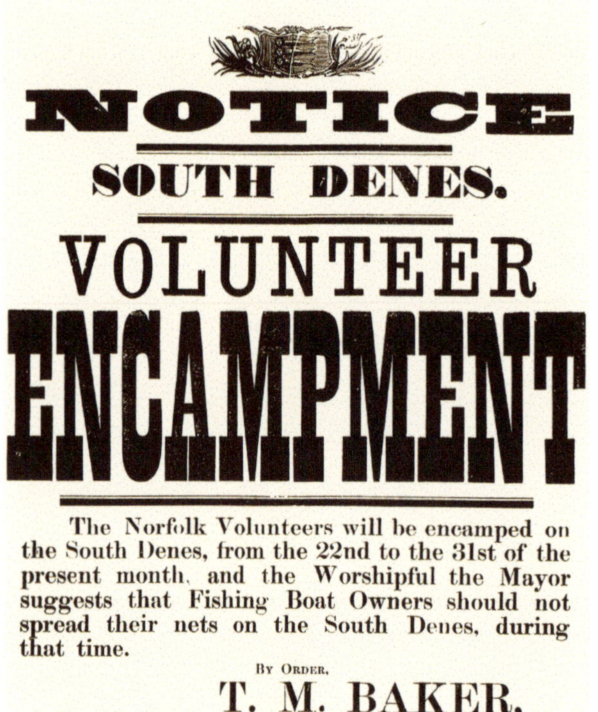

One of the notices to make sure the fishermen didn't spread their nets to dry on the South Denes, Great Yarmouth, during the Norfolk Volunteers encampment, July 1880.

similar lines – two regular battalions and one militia battalion. The rifle volunteers were also redesignated as volunteer battalions of the main county regiment.

Old barracks were enlarged and new volunteer drill halls erected, such as the Volunteer Artillery Drill Hall on Nelson Road, Great Yarmouth, which was built in 1881. The city of Norwich also felt that under the new army scheme the Norfolk Regiment should have a purpose-built home in the city itself. A suitable site was identified on Mousehold Heath and the citizens of Norwich raised £1,600 by public subscription for the Corporation to buy the site and land for access roads. The main blocks of Britannia Barracks were built in 1886–87 by Norwich City Council and presented to the Norfolk Regiment as its first permanent depot.

The South African War (1899–1902) saw both regular and volunteer battalion soldiers of the Norfolk Regiment proceed to active service. A detachment of the Norfolk Artillery Militia (approximately 142 men), the 43rd Company, 12th Battalion, Imperial Yeomanry raised by Colonel John Harvey were recruited from Norfolk and Suffolk. In the time-honoured fashion of recruiting parties, the recruiting station for Norfolk men volunteering to serve in the Imperial Yeomanry was The Maid's Head Hotel, Norwich.

The 310 Norfolk men who lost their lives in the conflict are commemorated on the South African War Memorial on Shirehall Plain in Norwich, which was unveiled by GOC Eastern District, Major-General Arthur Singleton Wynne on 17 November 1904.

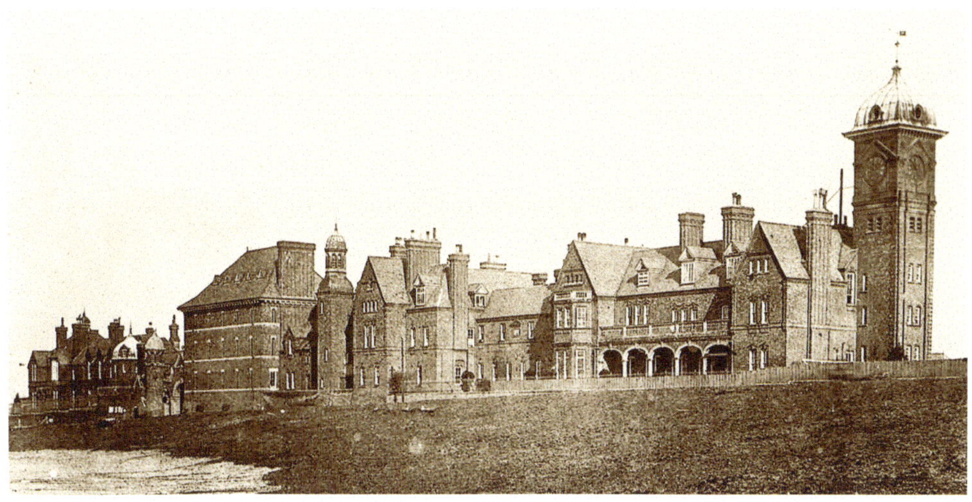

Britannia Barracks, Mousehold Heath, Norwich, *c.* 1910. Built by Norwich City Council in 1886–87, they were presented to the Norfolk Regiment as its first permanent depot.

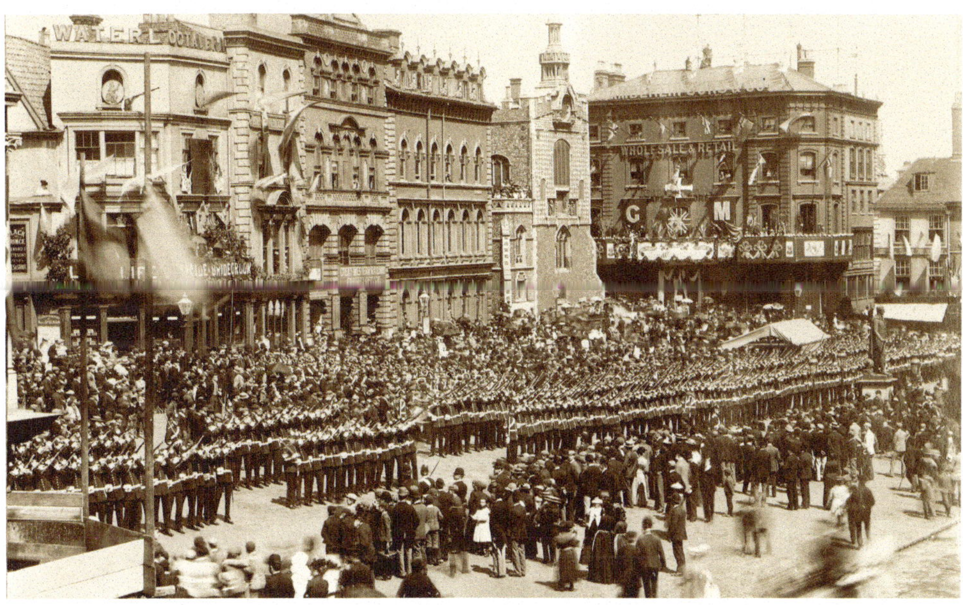

Members of the Norfolk Regiment Volunteer Battalions and Norfolk Artillery Volunteers firing the *feu de joie* in Norwich Market Place to celebrate the Duke of York's marriage in 1893.

Among the legacies of the South African War was the success of the mounted infantry units and Imperial Yeomanry in South Africa. This, coupled with Edward VII not liking the idea that Norfolk had not had a unit of county yeomanry for many years, led to a request from the king to Colonel Henry Barclay of Hanworth Hall to raise the Norfolk Yeomanry in 1901.

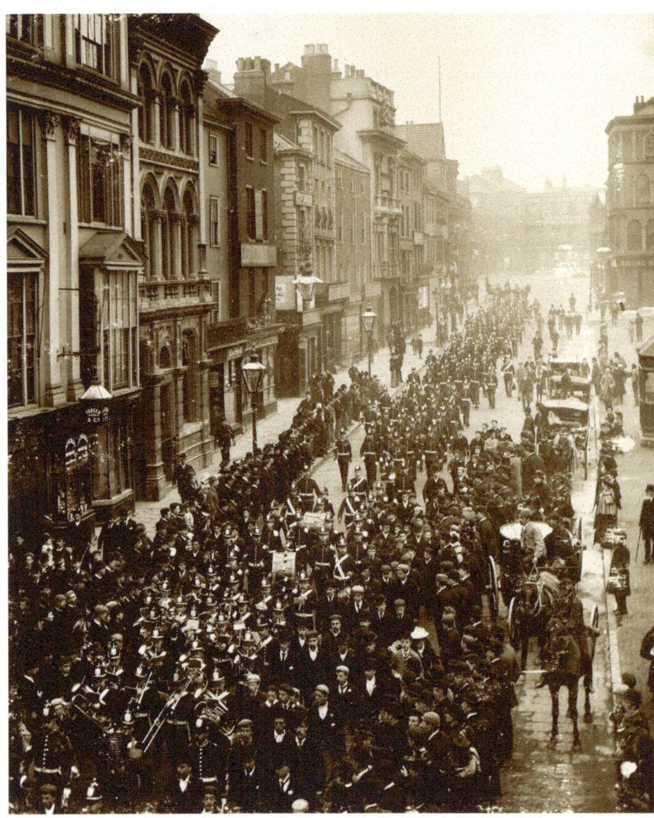

Left: The Norwich Batteries of the Norfolk Volunteer Artillery marching down Gentleman's Walk led by their band on Church Parade, Sunday 28 April 1895.

Below: Crew and ammunition limber of the 2nd Battery, 1st Norfolk Volunteer Artillery, ready for inspection on Mousehold, 1895.

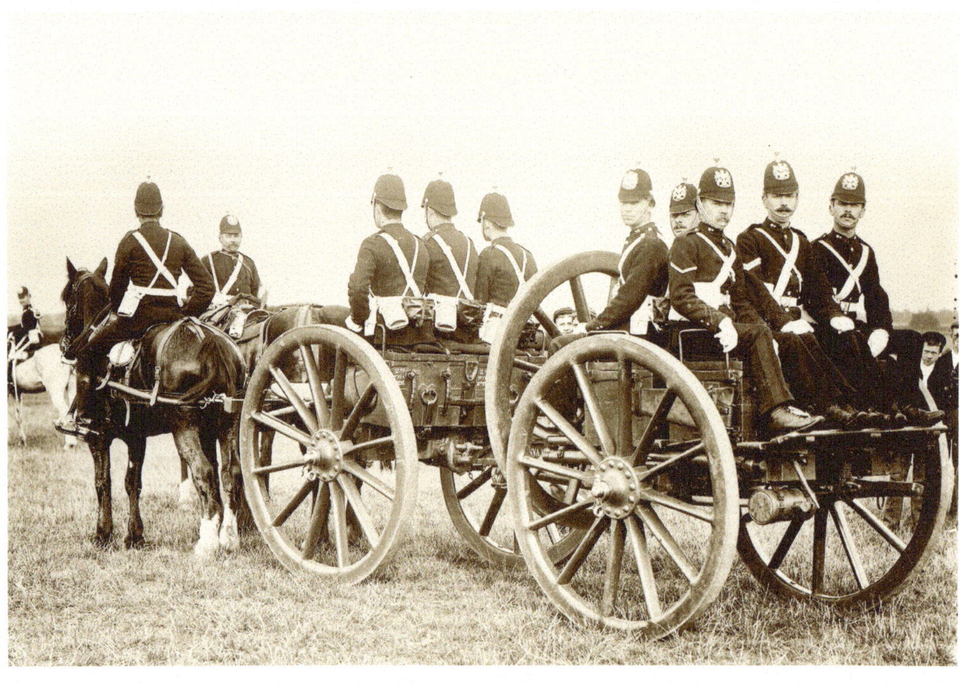

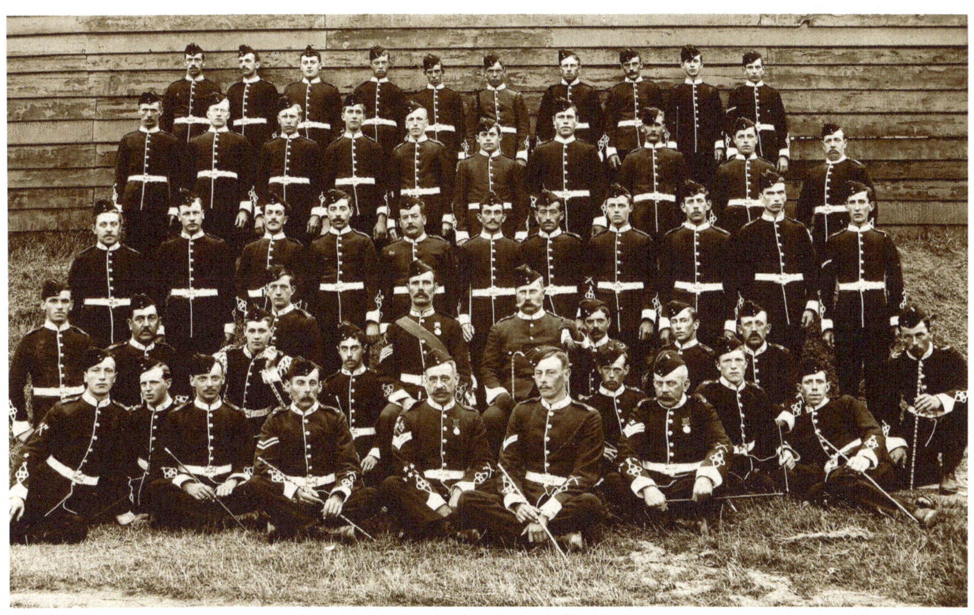

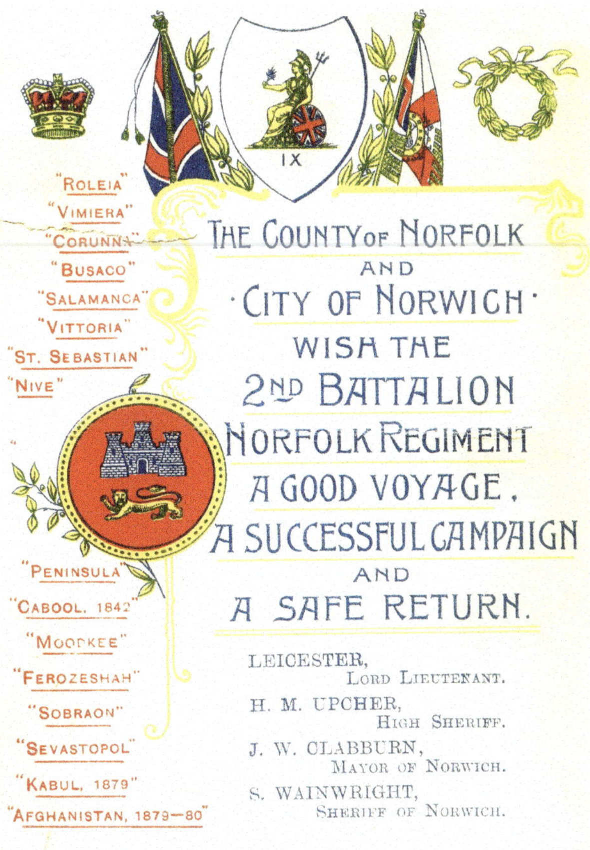

Above: G Company (Swaffham), 3rd Volunteer Battalion, the Norfolk Regiment, *c.* 1895.

Right: The good wishes card given to members of 2nd Battalion, the Norfolk Regiment, as they proceeded to the South African War in 1900.

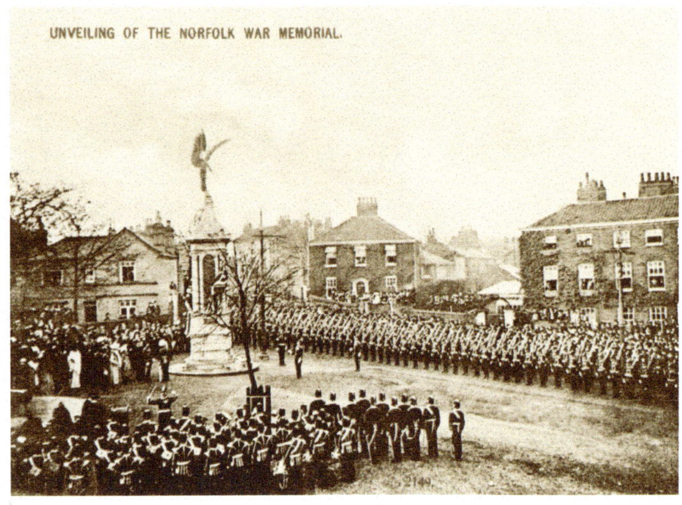

Unveiling of the Norfolk and Norwich South African War Memorial on Shirehall Plain, Norwich, by GOC Eastern District, Major-General Arthur Singleton Wynne on 17 November 1904.

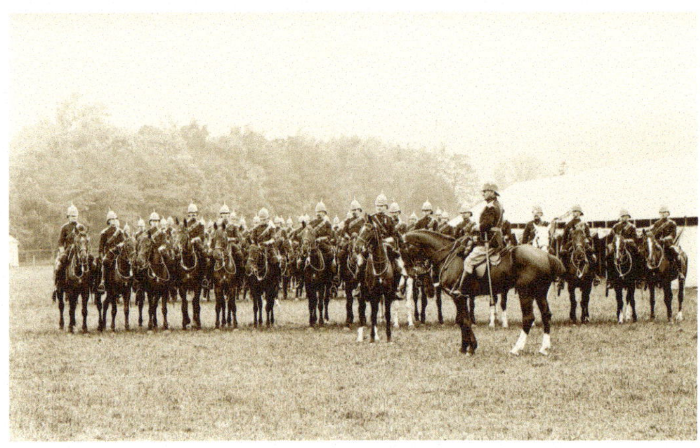

Norfolk Yeomanry Squadron Parade, Cromer, 1903. They are still wearing their first style of uniforms with colonial pattern helmets with spikes.

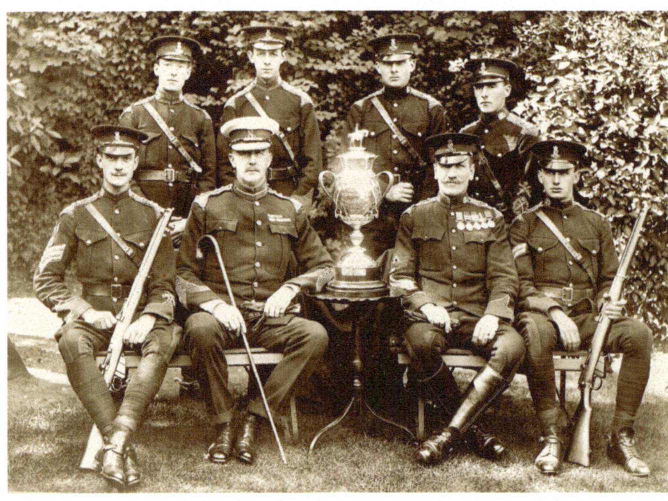

Colonel H. A. Barclay, seated centre left, and the Norfolk Yeomanry shooting team that won the Mander Cup at Bisley, 1909.

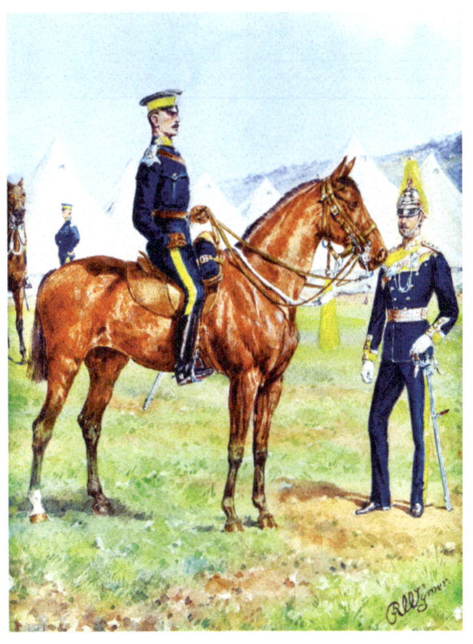 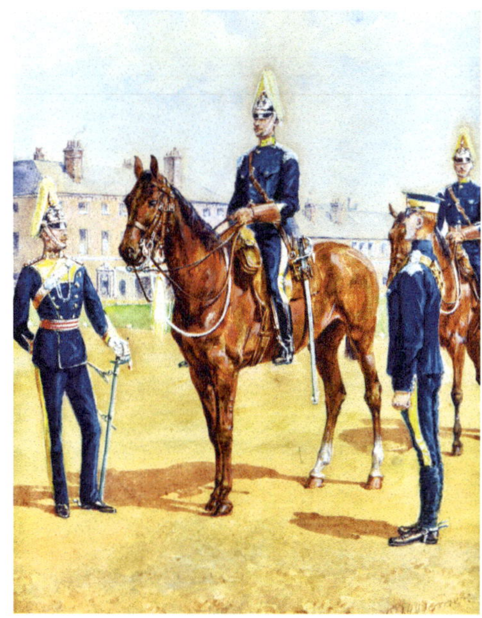

Above left: Painting showing the mounted and dismounted review order uniforms of the Norfolk Yeomanry, *c.* 1910.

Above right: Painting showing uniforms of the full dress and mounted review order of Norfolk Yeomanry, *c.* 1910.

Times were changing for Britain's armed forces in the first decade of the twentieth century, and Norfolk men were at the vanguard of the improvements and innovations for the Royal Navy. When made First Sea Lord, Admiral Sir John Fisher of Kilverston Hall led the push to persuade the War Office, and ultimately the government, that investment in the first iron-clad, big-gun, turbine-driven battleship would be worthwhile. Among his staunchest supporters was Admiral Sir Arthur Knyvet Wilson VC of Swaffham, a career naval officer who made a significant contribution to the Royal Navy through his own innovations for torpedoes and submarines. Thanks to their drive and support the revolutionary HMS *Dreadnought* entered service in 1906. *Dreadnought* represented such a marked advance in naval technology that all other existing battleships were rendered obsolete. Henceforward, all surface navies would be measured by their dreadnought strength – Britannia literally ruled the waves.

The British Army was also modernised under a rolling programme implemented by Secretary of State for War Richard Burden Haldane. It began with Officers Training Corps (OTC) in public schools to provide a seedbed of future officers. A British Expeditionary Force (BEF) that could be created from home-based regular battalions in the event of a war emergency was organised and the old volunteer system was abolished in favour of a new Territorial Force (TF). The idea being that if the regular battalions were deployed abroad as a BEF, the Territorial Force would be mobilised to defend Britain. The TF was not created with any intention that it would be deployed overseas.

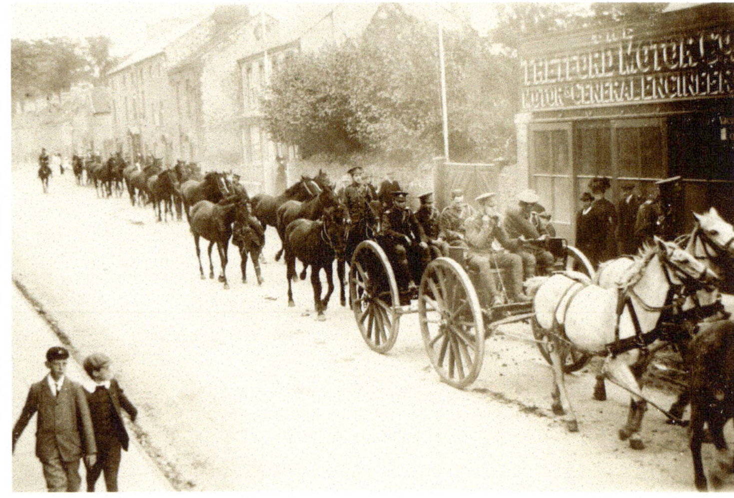

Members of 1st East Anglian Brigade, Royal Field Artillery, leaving Thetford Camp, September 1911.

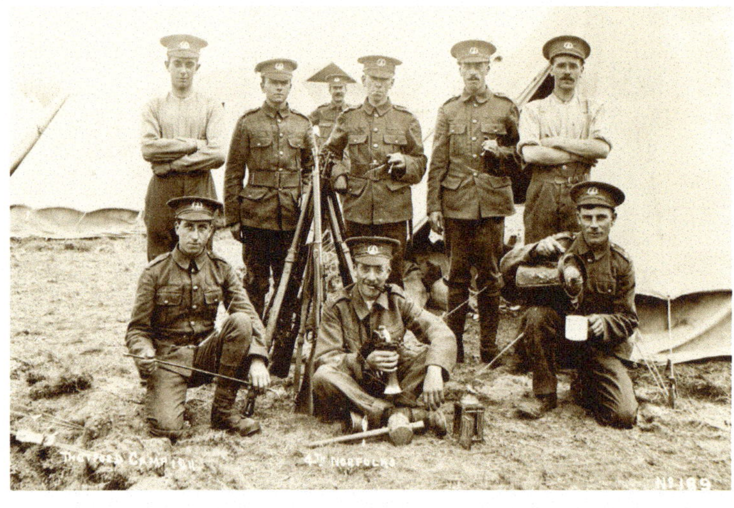

Some of the lads of 4th Battalion, the Norfolk Regiment (TF), at Thetford Camps in 1911.

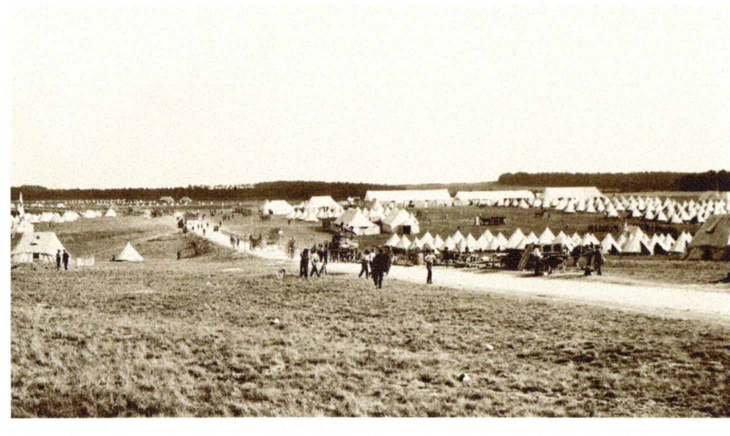

Norfolk territorial infantry and corps at Thetford Camp 1911.

In the days before television, being a part-time soldier in the Territorial Force was just as much of a pastime as playing sports. Sections, platoons, companies and battalions could be found across the county filled with local lads, extended family members, friends and workmates. There were regular drill nights, inter-company sports, days shooting at the range, regular camps and manoeuvres at weekends, as such these lads were soon nicknamed 'Saturday Night Soldiers'.

The Great Manoeuvres of 1912

In 1912 the eastern counties of England played host to military manoeuvres of an unprecedented scale. The forces were nearly equal in size. The staff of the Red Army

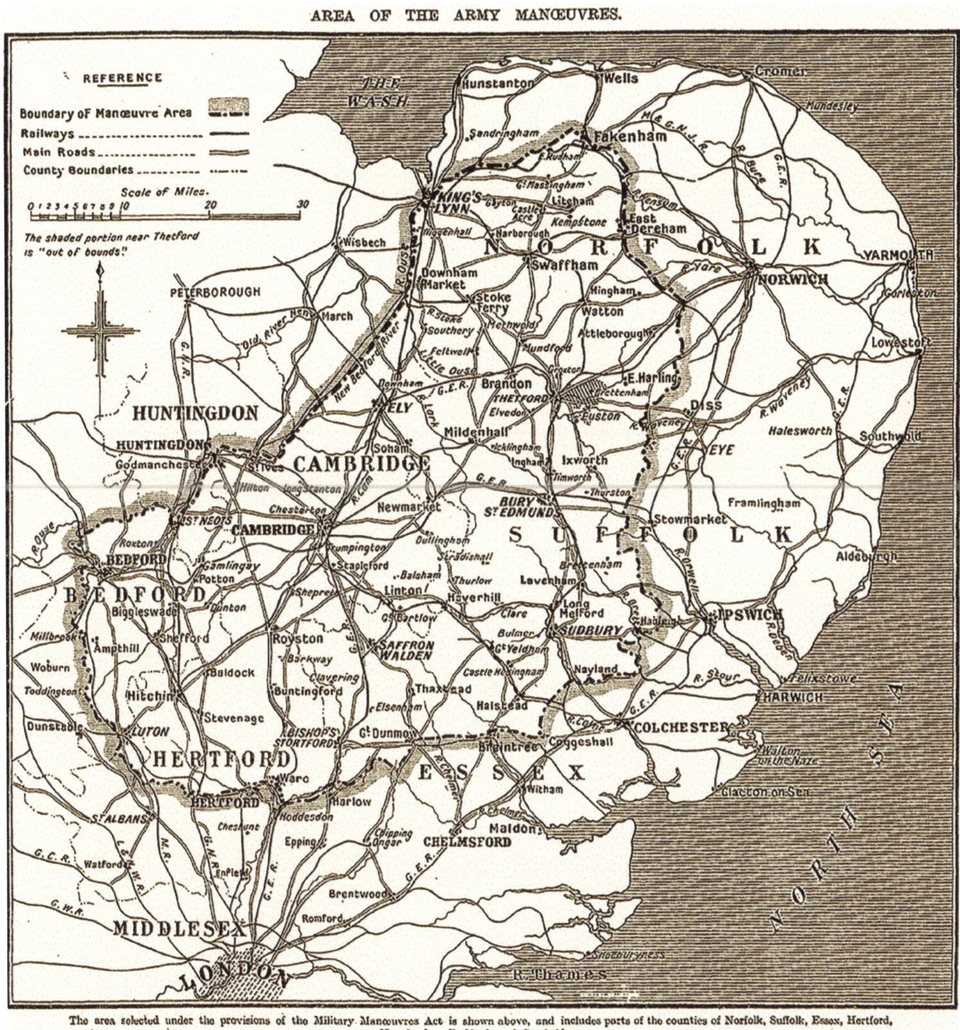

Map of the unprecidented 'Great Manoeuvres' that took place across the whole of East Anglia during August and September 1912.

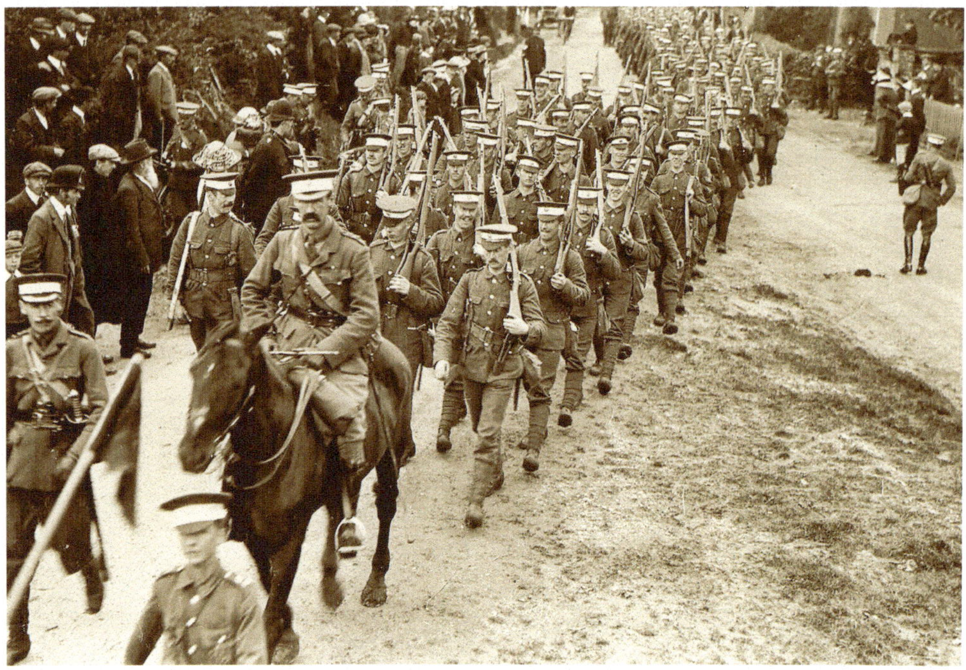

Officers and men of the Coldstream Guards moving out from Swaffham during 'the Great Manoeuvres' of 1912.

under General Haig were Aldershot command, who were accustomed to working together. In contrast, the Blue Army under General Sir James Grierson were drawn from all commands, except Aldershot, with two brigades drawn from Household Cavalry, Scots Greys, Yeomanry and Cyclists. The Blue Infantry came from the Southern Command (3rd Division), Eastern Command (4th Division) and the Territorial Force. The main concentration of troops in Norfolk was in Swaffham, with over 2,000 Red troops predominantly from 2nd and 3rd Grenadier Guards and 2nd Coldstream Guards. All ranks and services were included; the total number of troops involved across East Anglia amounted to nearly 50,000. The scenario was that the Blue Army invaded and the Red Army defended. Blues won.

During the manoeuvres it was soon apparent that Haig had not realised the importance of the spotter aircraft. Grierson, the victorious commander of the Blue Army, had hidden his troops from observation and Haig had failed to ascertain their movements or deployment. In contrast, Grierson had used his spotters well and had almost perfect knowledge of the movements of Haig's troops. In the final analysis of the manoeuvres, despite the efforts of the umpires and judges to make the contest appear more even, Haig who had the odds in his favour was decisively beaten by Grierson. You may wonder why we did not hear much more of Grierson during the First World War; he tragically died of an aneurysm of the heart on a train near Amiens on 17 August 1914.

7. The First World War

As the storm clouds of war gathered, Norfolk stood ready. During the weekend of 1–2 August 1914 a palpable military presence was felt along the Norfolk coast and in Norwich as soldiers were posted to guard key areas such as railway stations, utilities, wireless stations and military installations. The Admiralty ordered a calling up of all classes of navy reserves, which reached some towns as early as 4 a.m. on Sunday 2 August. The Territorial Forces were poised to act, so when the declaration of war was made at 11 p.m. on 4 August 1914 the navy was ready and the military forces of Norfolk were mobilised.

Lord Kitchener, the newly appointed Secretary of State for War, believed the country should prepare itself for a period of at least three years of conflict that would require some seventy divisions to fight it. Recruitment opened for his first 100,000 men on 11 August. Hundreds of Norfolk men answered their country's call in August 1914, but there were also many who saw the army pay – 1s a day – and decided that they would earn better money getting the harvest in first. The military authorities soon picked up on this and geared up a massive recruiting campaign in agricultural areas around the country in September 1914, once the harvests were in. It yielded the greatest numbers of volunteer soldiers joining up from such areas during the war – an average 33,000 recruits were enlisting on a daily basis nationwide.

It is often assumed that all Norfolk men served in the Norfolk Regiment, but this is far from the truth. Many lads did indeed serve with their brothers and friends in the Regular, Territorial and Service battalions of their county regiment, but there were a further four companies for the New Army raised in the spring of 1915 after appeals for skilled tradesmen – such as blacksmiths, farriers, carpenters, electricians and telegraph

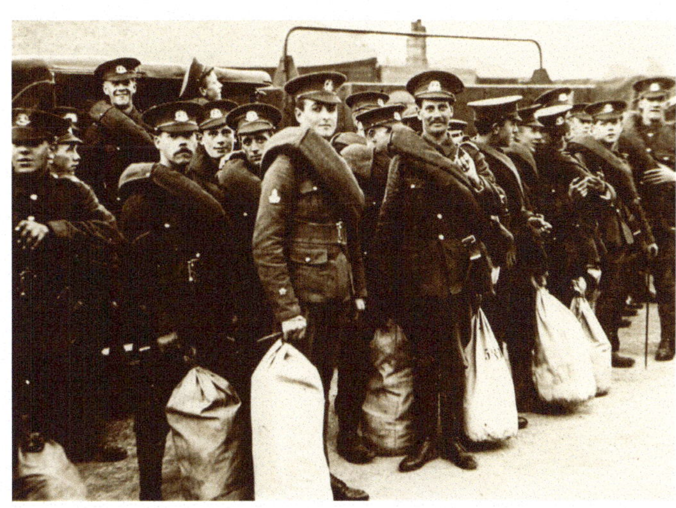

Some of the King's Lynn Company, 5th Battalion. The Norfolk Regiment are making ready to leave from King's Lynn station to report to Battalion Headquarters at East Dereham on the day they were mobilised for war, 5 August 1914.

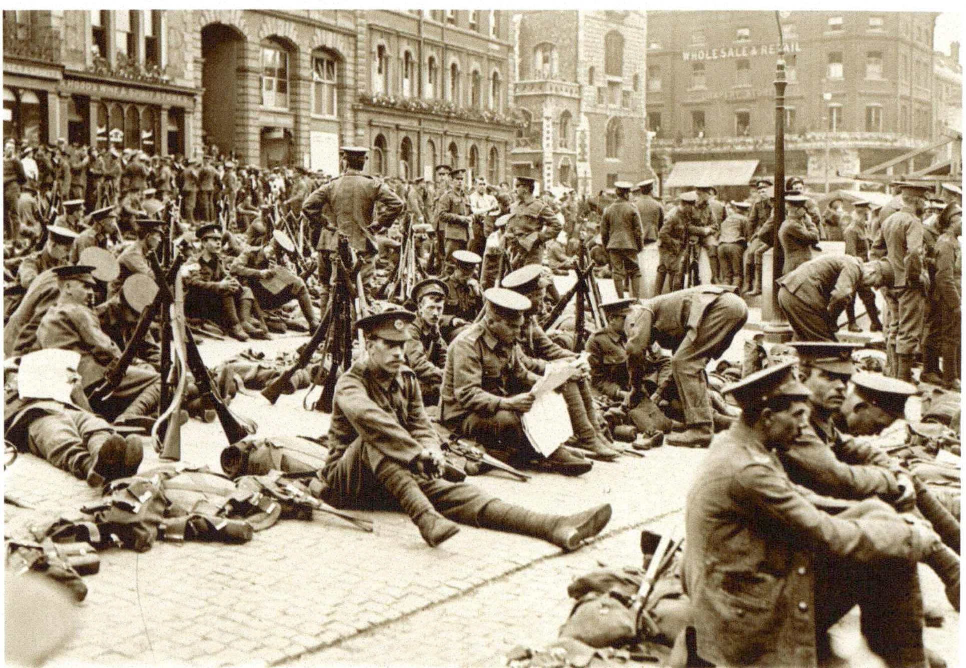

The first major arrival of troops to Norfolk from outside the county in the First World War were 2nd Battalion, the Essex Regiment, pictured in Norwich Market Place, 10 August 1914.

operators – were made by Dr Gordon Munn, Lord Mayor of Norwich. The aim was to make a unit of skilled men to serve together in an engineers' unit. As a result the 207th, 208th and 209th Field Companies and Royal Engineers of the 34th Division were all raised from local men. There was also the Norfolk Yeomanry and TF Corps troops, such as 2nd East Anglian Field Ambulance, Royal Army Medical Corps, that served in the 54th (East Anglian) Division in Gallipoli. In 1915 they were joined in the division by 1st East Anglian Brigade Royal Field Artillery that went on to campaign in Palestine in 1917. There were also many men who thought they would see a little more of the country when they enlisted and chose regiments from counties miles from home, while others were asked to do so by parents concerned about having all their sons in the same battalion. After conscription was introduced in 1916 Norfolk men were sent to a huge variety of regiments on call-up or after training.

Fears of invasion were very real in 1914 and yeomanry from the 1st and 2nd Mounted Divisions (many of them from the Midlands and Wales) were drafted to Norfolk as coastal patrol and rapid-response troops. Local emergency committees were also formed to put in place evacuation procedures and establish an emergency corps to help in the evacuation of the local population, destroy things that may help the enemy, assemble barricades and dig trenches. Out of these schemes came the first bands of men who armed themselves and planned to defend their villages and towns. Authorities were not keen on this idea without regulation so the Volunteer Training Corps scheme was introduced – very much a forerunner of the Home Guard of the Second World War. Members were recruited from

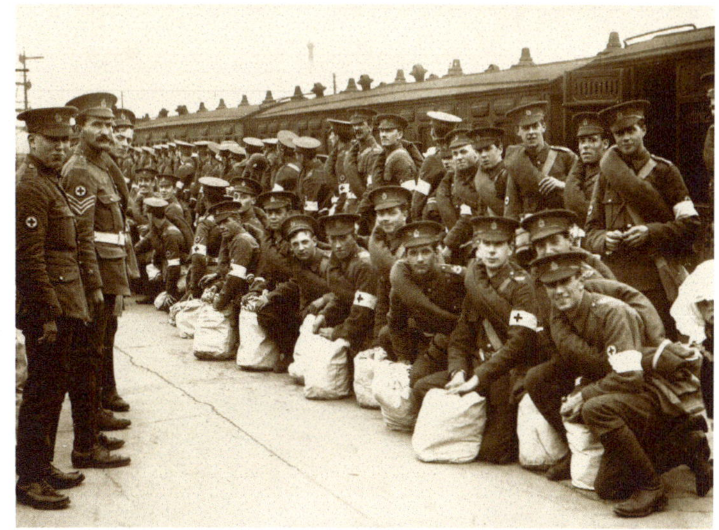

Men of 2nd East Anglian Field Ambulance departing for their war stations from Norwich in 1914. They would service with 54th (East Anglian) Division in Gallipoli, Egypt and Palestine during the war.

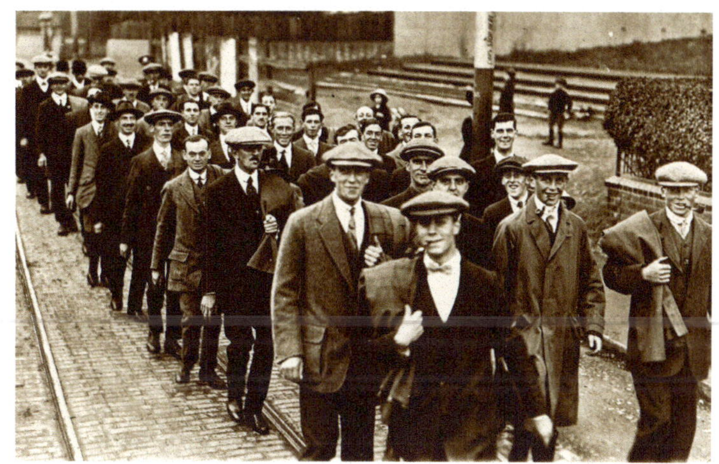

New recruits for Kitchener's Army marching on a Norwich street, 1914.

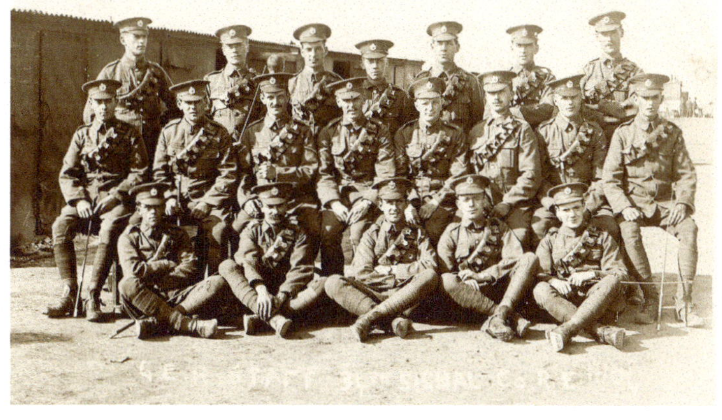

Members of the Great Eastern Railway from Norfolk serving in the Norwich raised 34th Division Signal Company, Royal Engineers 1915.

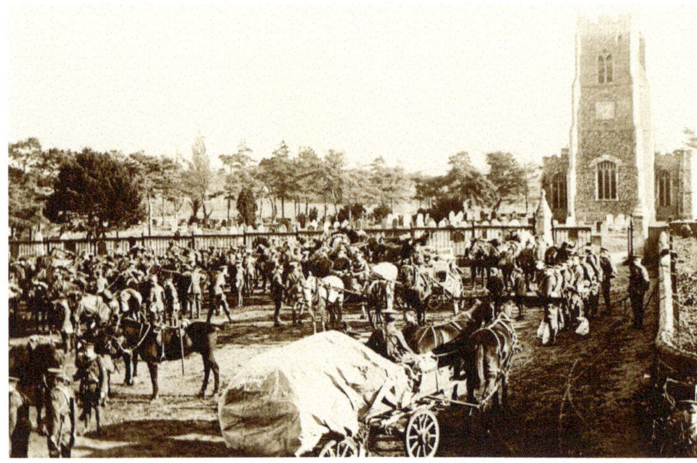

Members of the Cheshire Yeomanry, their mounts and transport shortly after their arrival at Church Plain, Loddon, 1914.

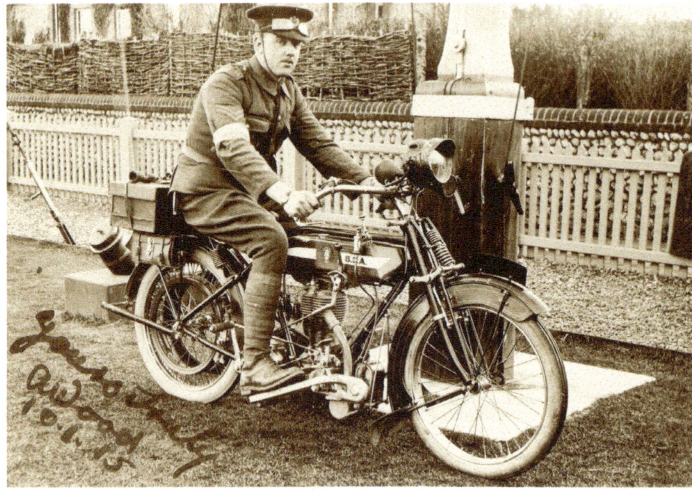

Royal Engineers Despatch Rider outside the Coastguard Station, Cromer, in 1915. These were part of the cycle, motorcycle and horse-mounted troops deployed along the Norfolk coast on anti-invasion defences and patrols, 1914–15.

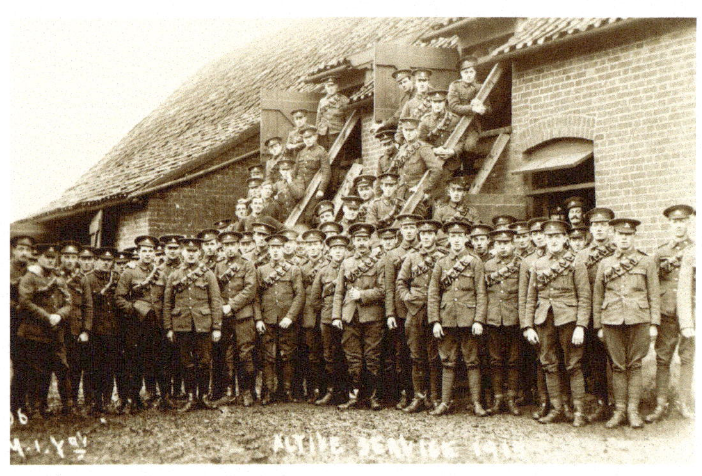

Men of the Montgomeryshire Yeomanry at Aylsham in 1915, one of a number of Welsh Yeomanry units despatched to Norfolk as part of the 1st and 2nd Yeomanry Divisions during the invasion scares of 1914–15.

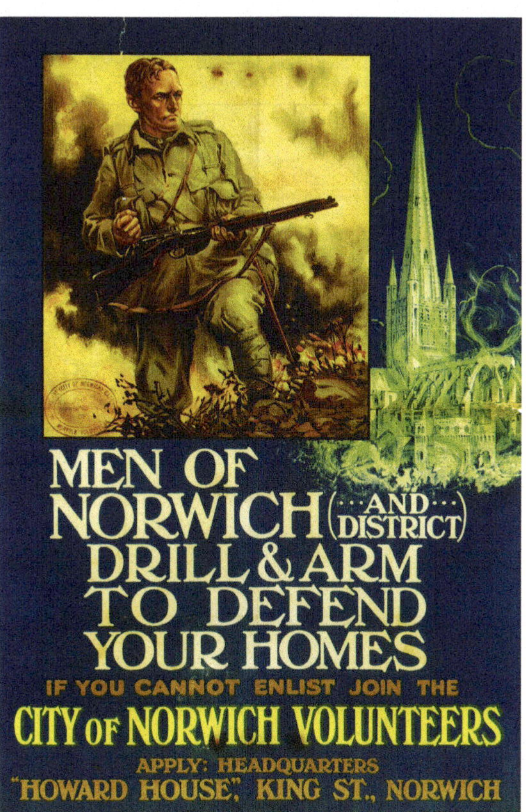

Dramatic recruiting poster for the City of Norwich Volunteers, the First World War forerunner of the Home Guard.

local men too old to serve in the military or those in war-reserved occupations to train to defend their local areas. By 1915 they were issued rifles, uniformed and brought together in two main units, the Norfolk Volunteers (for the defence of the county) and the City of Norwich Volunteers.

Bombardments

Norfolk became the first British county to suffer bombardment from the sea during the First World War when, early on the misty morning of Tuesday 3 November 1914, Great Yarmouth was shelled by battlecruisers of the 1st and 2nd Scouting Groups of the Imperial German Navy. Fortunately the shells fell short and there were no casualties. The town was attacked again on Tuesday 25 April 1916; this time it was a miracle that no one was hurt. On Monday 14 January 1918 Great Yarmouth was shelled by German warships for the last time. Some twenty shells found their mark, houses and buildings were damaged, windows were blown in, eight people were injured and four killed.

The Zeppelin Menace

The first Zeppelin raid on Great Britain was conducted over Norfolk on the evening of 19 January 1915. Zeppelins L3 under the command of Kapitänleutnant Hans Fritz and L4 under Kapitänleutnant Count Magnus von Platen-Hallermund made landfall near

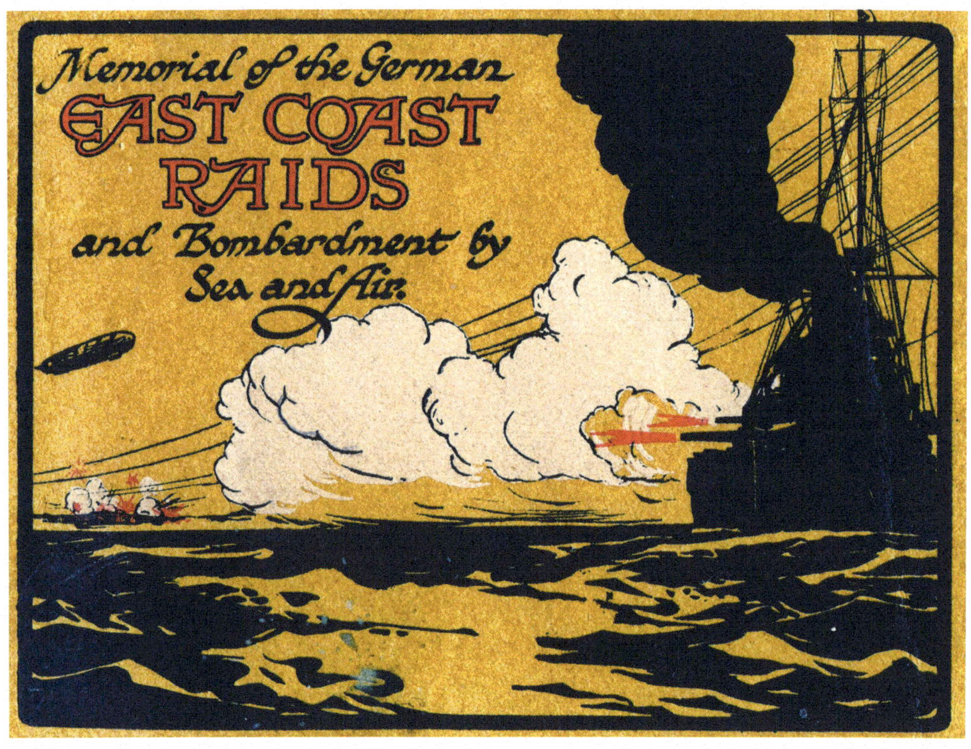

Cover of the booklet charting the bombardments and Zeppelin air raids on the east coast of England, first produced in 1915.

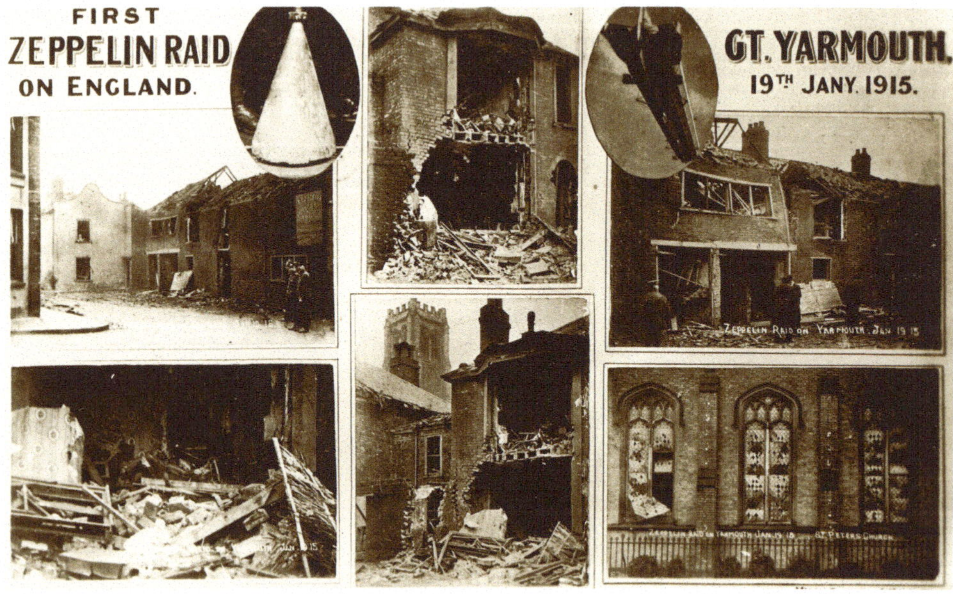

Postcard produced after the Zeppelin raid on Great Yarmouth, showing one of the unexploded bombs and some of the damage inflicted on the town on 19 January 1915.

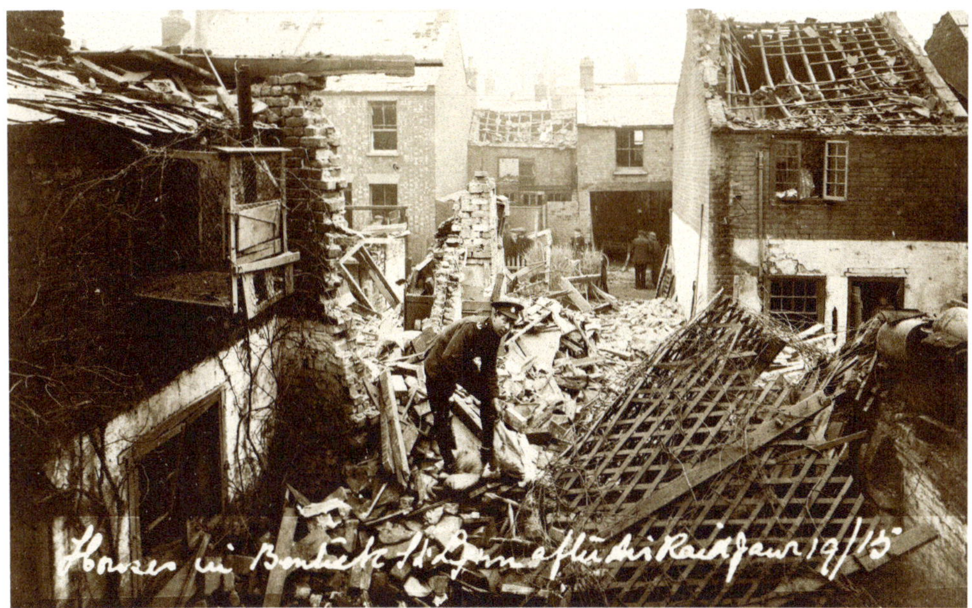

A soldier picks through the wreckage and indicates the blood-stained mattress of Percy Goate (fourteen) who died of shock on Bentick Street, King's Lynn, during the Zeppelin raid of 19 January 1915. The other fatality of the raid was war widow Mrs Alice Maud Gazley (twenty-six) who also died of shock while sheltering with friends in the house next door.

Bacton. The L3 turned south-east and went on to bomb Yarmouth, where cobbler Samuel Smith and elderly spinster Martha Taylor were killed on St Peter's Plain. Meanwhile, the L4 turned to follow the coastline towards the west, dropping bombs on Snettisham, Heacham, Hunstanton and King's Lynn, where young war widow Alice Maud Gazely and fourteen-year-old Percy Goate were killed and many more were wounded.

Zeppelin raiders regularly passed over Norfolk during the war and occasionally dropped bombs, causing more damage and deaths. The worst loss of life suffered during an air raid on the county occurred on the evening of Wednesday 9 September 1915 when Zeppelin L14 under the command of Kapitänleutnant Alois Böcker dropped a number of bombs on East Dereham, causing serious damage around the Church Street area, killing three and fatally injuring two soldiers.

Efforts to combat the Zeppelin menace began immediately after the first attack. The Royal Naval Mobile Anti-Aircraft Brigade was despatched under Lieutenant Mackenzie Ashton to North Norfolk with searchlights, armoured cars and mobile anti-aircraft guns. The Royal Naval Air Station at South Denes, Great Yarmouth, was sent Bristol Scout 'D' aircraft specifically to conduct anti-Zeppelin patrols. Sea planes and flying boats were also sent to patrol the North Sea for enemy shipping. The RNAS station also had a number of satellite airfields – often referred to as 'Night Landing Grounds' – along and slightly inland from the coast at Narborough, Sedgeford, Holt (Bayfield), Bacton, Burgh Castle, Aldeburgh and Covehithe. In 1916 marker buoys were placed on Hickling Broad to provide an emergency landing place for the station's seaplanes and flying boats.

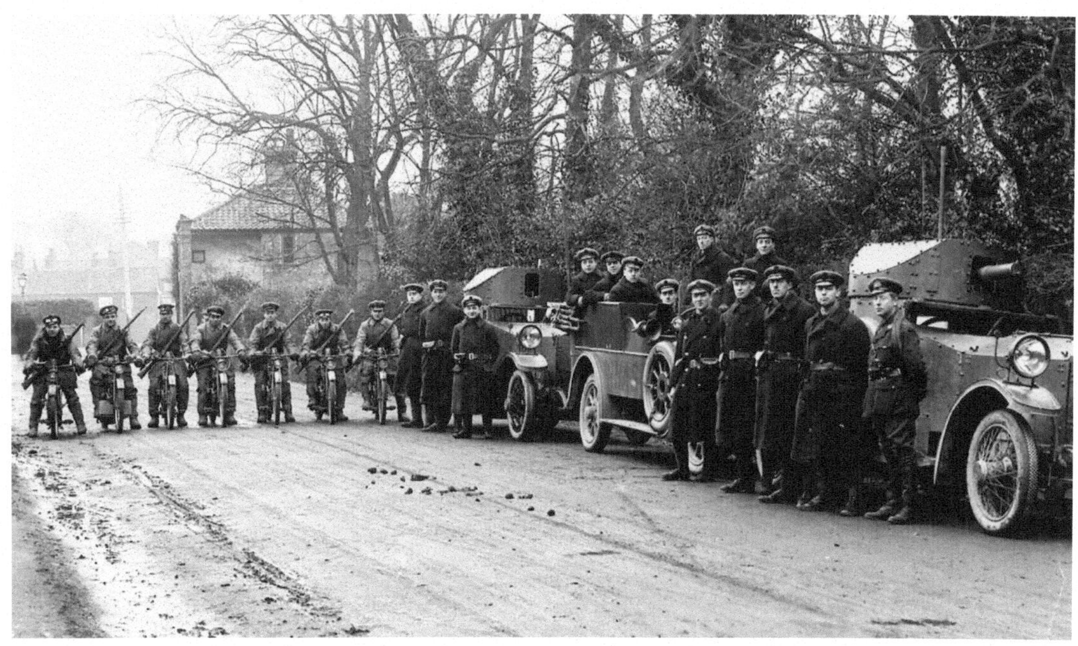

The Royal Naval Air Service Mobile Anti-Aircraft Brigade deployed to the north-east coast of Norfolk on anti-Zeppelin duties pictured at North Walsham (where they were based), 1915.

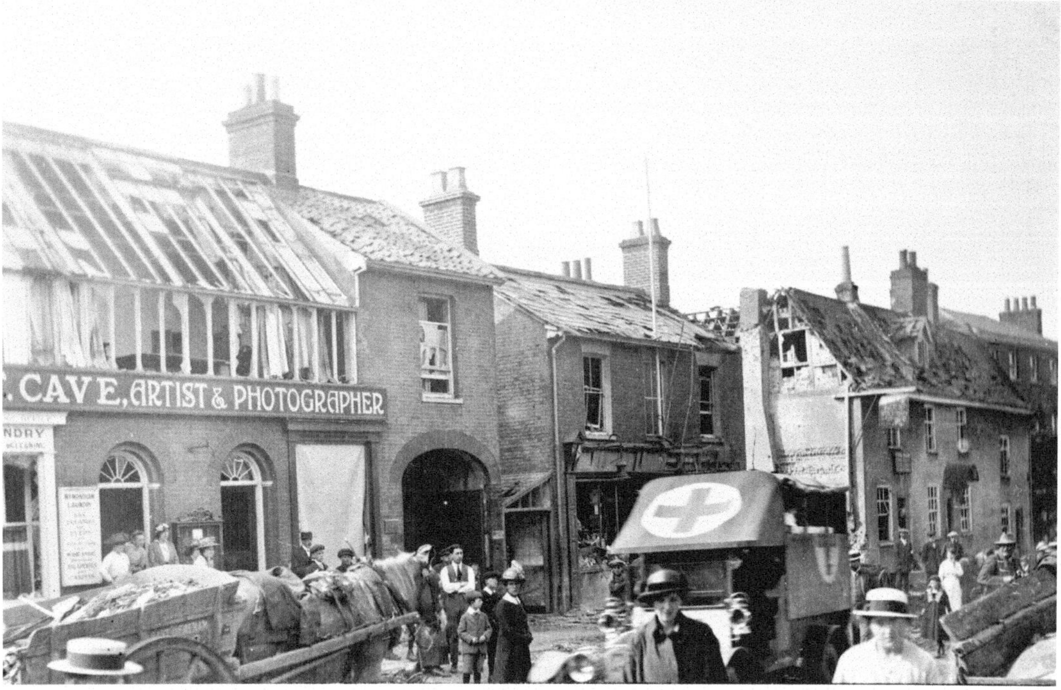

The wrecked houses and businesses on Church Street, East Dereham, after the Zeppelin raid of 9 September 1915.

Some of the Norfolk landing grounds became airfields in their own right such as Bacton and, notably, Narborough, which was given up by the RNAS and taken on by the Royal Flying Corps in April 1916, growing to cover a site of some 908 acres and becoming (with the exception of four airship stations) the largest aerodrome in Britain. The RFC also developed airfields and landing grounds used by Norfolk-based squadrons at Earsham, Freethorpe, Gooderstone Warren, Mousehold Heath, Saxthorpe, Sedgeford (taken over from RNAS by RFC in 1916 but still used as a landing field by RNAS Yarmouth until 1918), Sporle, Tottenhill, Bircham Newton, Feltwell, Harling Road, Hingham, Marham, Mattishall, Thetford and West Rudham. A second RNAS airfield was opened in 1916 at Pulham as a naval airship base, flying mostly coastal-type blimps on patrols over an area that extended from Margate to Dunkirk in the south and from Mablethorpe to Holland in the north. These stubby little airships were soon nicknamed 'Pulham Pigs'.

The last Zeppelin to be shot down in Britain during the First World War was the L70, containing Peter Strasser, head of the Imperial German Naval Airship Division. It was brought down by Major Egbert Cadbury and Captain Robert Leckie flying a DH-4 from the RNAS base at Great Yarmouth on 5 August 1918. The L70 came down around 8 miles just north of Wells-next-the-Sea. A search of the sea soon revealed none of the crew had survived. Both Cadbury and Leckie were recognised for this action with the award of the Distinguished Flying Cross.

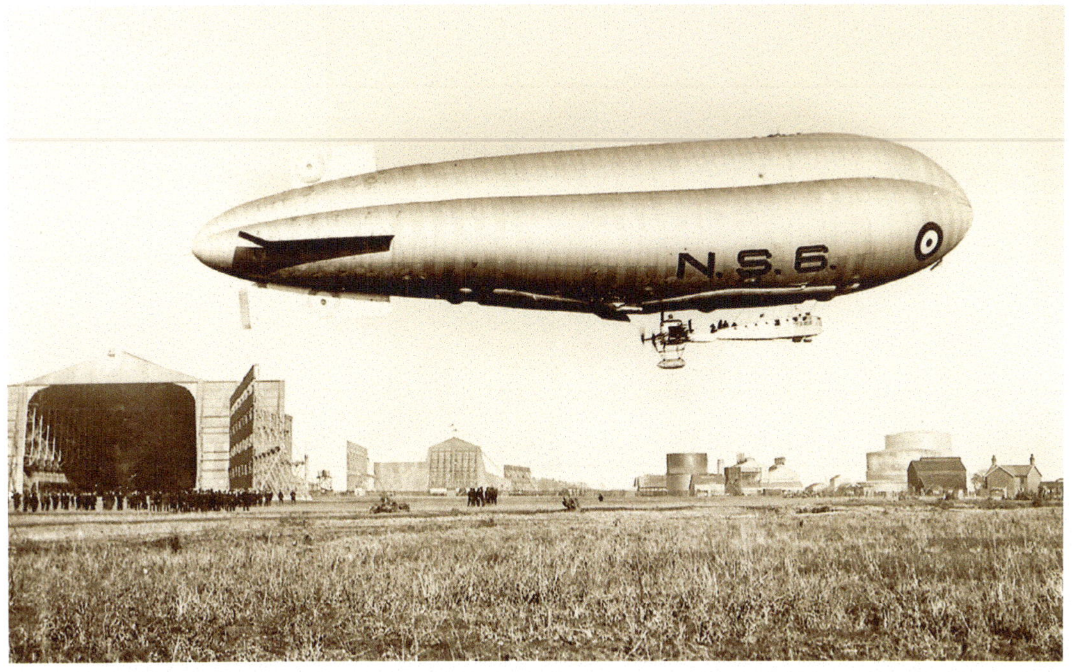

The Pulham Royal Naval Airship Service Station, pictured shortly after it became operational in 1916. In the foreground is NS6, a blimp used for patrolling the coast to spot enemy shipping movements. To the locals these stubby airships were known as 'Pulham Pigs'.

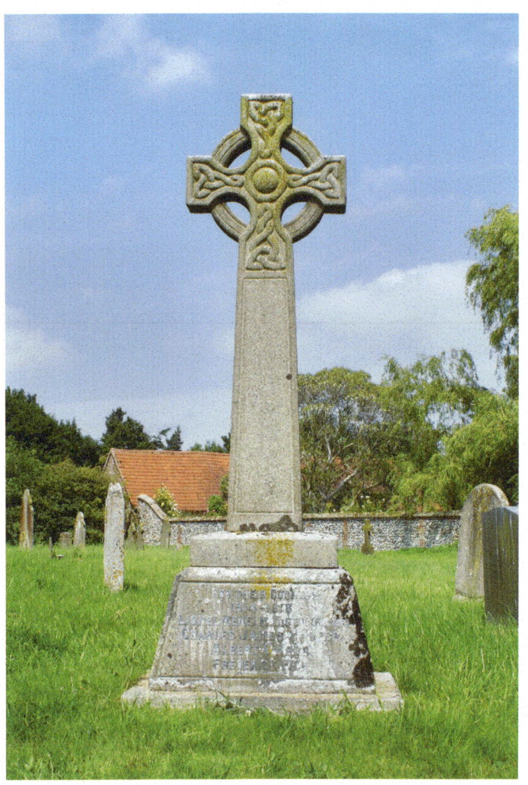

Wellingham War Memorial in Norfolk is unique in the county because it bears the name of a civilian killed in a Zeppelin air raid. Fredrick Pile (forty-five) was a farm labourer who lost his life after a bomb was dropped near him as he was running along the road to warn his employer of the impending danger on the night of 24 May 1917.

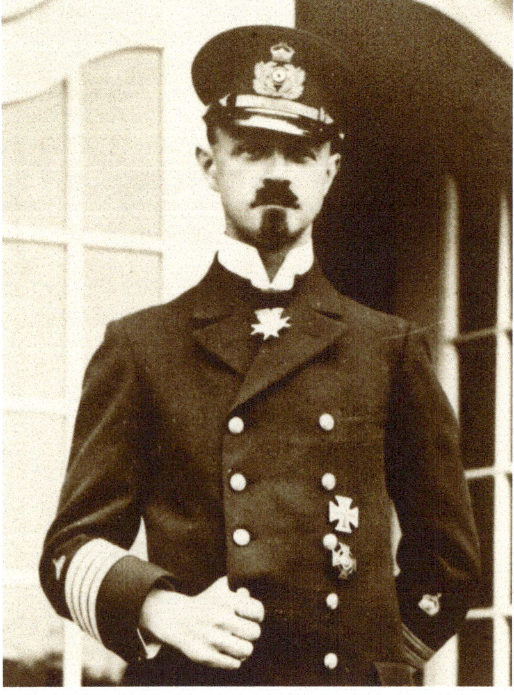

Peter Strasser, head of the Imperial German Naval Airship Division, was aboard the L70, the last Zeppelin to be shot down in Britain during the First World War, 8 miles north of Wells-next-the-Sea on 5 August 1918.

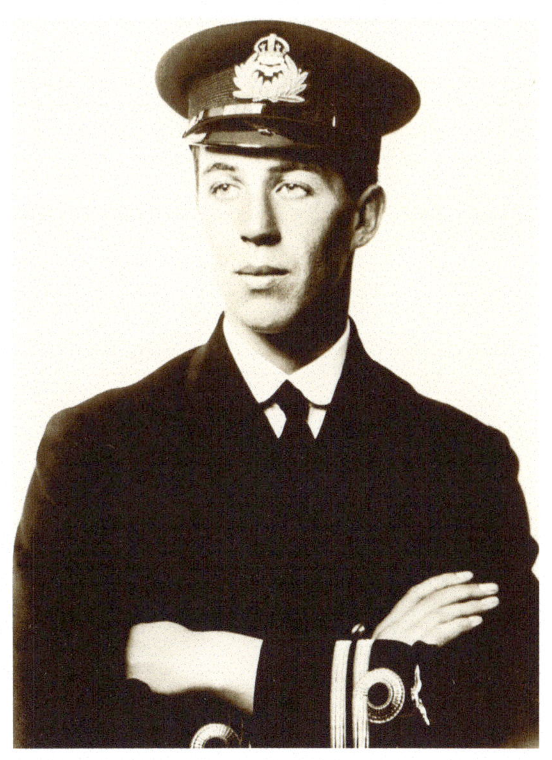

Right: Major Egbert Cadbury, RNAS, the pilot of the DH-4 that flew out from RNAS Great Yarmouth and brought down Zeppelin L70. Cadbury and the gunner Captain Robert Leckie were both awarded Distinguished Flying Crosses for the deed.

Below: First World War concrete block round pillbox, Aylmerton. Some of the first pillboxes ever constructed in Britain were built along the course of the River Ant and at key defensive points along the coast and across Norfolk during the period 1916–18.

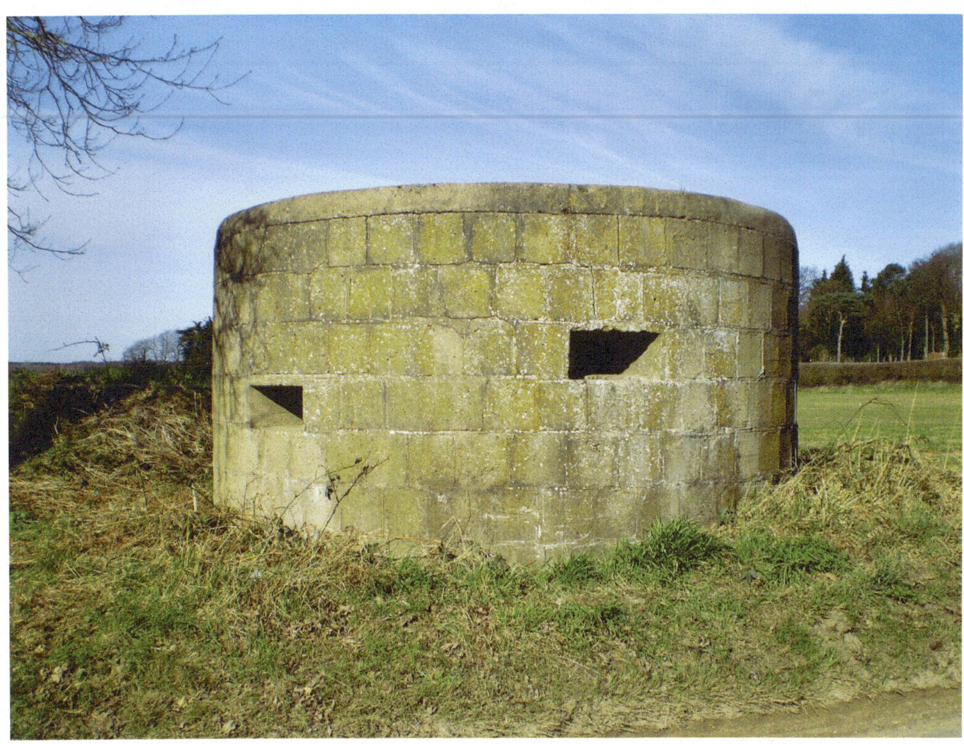

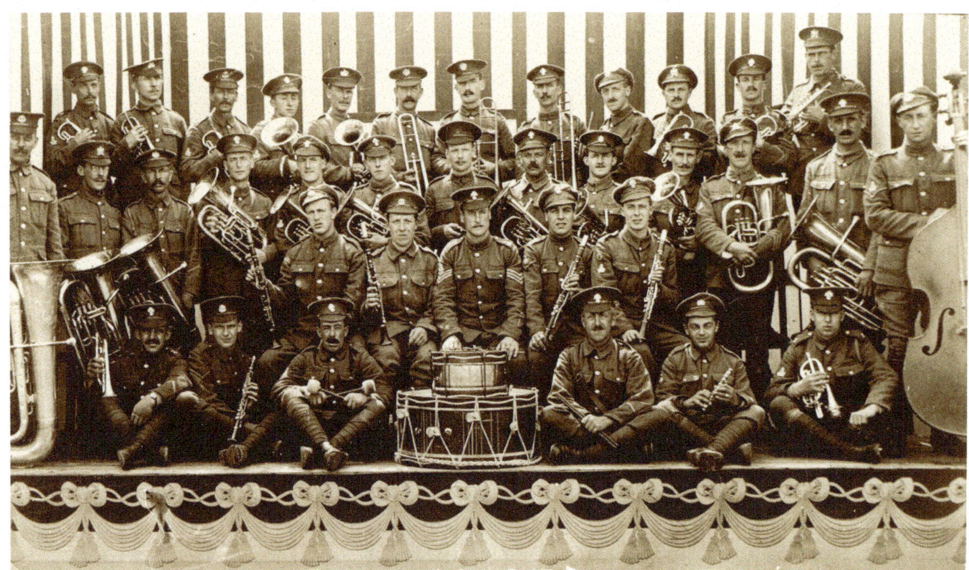

The Eastern Command Labour Centre Band, Thetford, 1917. Many wounded soldiers discharged from hospitals and soldiers who were deemed unfit for front-line service were sent to labour centres where they were often employed building military camps, defences and roads.

Women 'Did Their Bit' Too!

In 1914 there were sixty-four British Red Cross Society Voluntary Aid Detachments in Norfolk, and more followed soon after. Their main function was to train volunteers and provide staff for auxiliary war hospitals that opened in large private residences and public buildings across the county for convalescent wounded and sick soldiers. They also helped in the county war hospitals, and male members supplied a transport company to move wounded soldiers brought by train into the county to the hospitals where they would receive the care they needed. The first trainload of returned wounded soldiers to arrive in Norfolk pulled into Thorpe station, Norwich, on 29 September 1914. Over the next four years a total of sixty-two auxiliary war hospitals opened in the county, which provided 1,377 beds. A total of 27,446 convalescent soldiers passed through, who were cared for by 35,736 VAD nurses, orderlies, drivers and volunteers.

Women also ran fundraising collections and events for war charities, they set up working parties to make comforts such as scarves, socks and balaclavas for soldiers and sailors on active service, and they sent parcels of food, sweets and cigarettes to prisoners of war. As more and more men left to serve abroad local women replaced them in their jobs. They took on new work in many roles that would have been unthinkable for them before the war, from driving trams to making all manner of things for munitions – from fuses at Norwich Components to aircraft parts at Savages of Lynn. They made entire aircraft at Mann Egerton or Boulton & Paul Ltd in Norwich, who made 2,530 aircraft, notably FE 2Bs, Sopwith Camels and Snipes, and crafted a further 7,835 propellers in their Norwich factories. Also in the city, Barnards Ltd Engineers produced over 6,994 miles of wire netting for the War Office and Admiralty and hundreds of prefabricated wooden

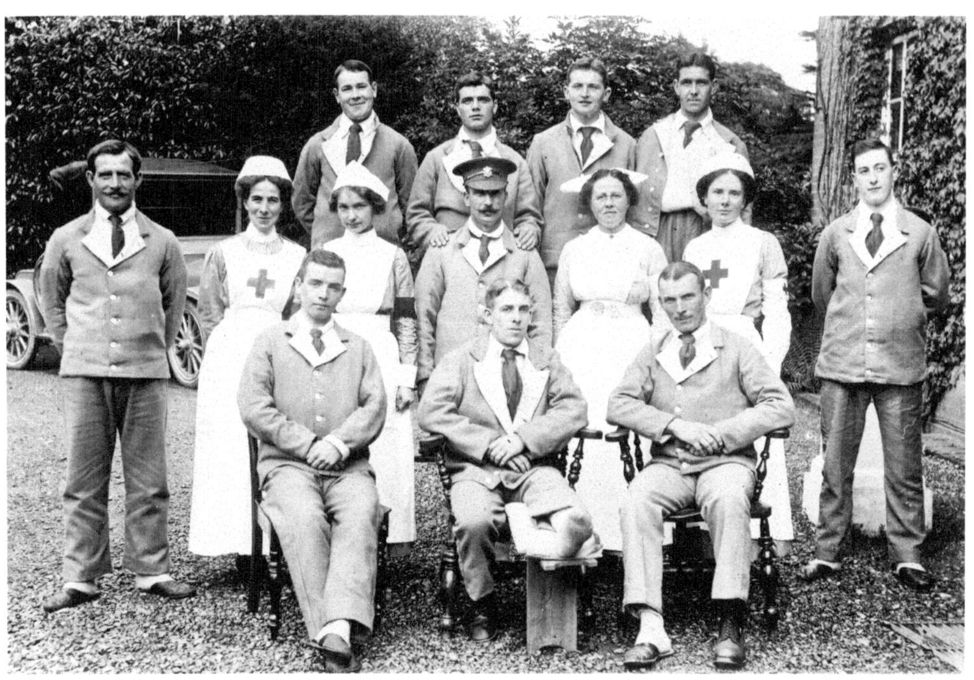

Qualified Nurse (centre right) and VAD Nurses with convalescent soldiers at the Brundall House Auxiliary War Hospital, 1916.

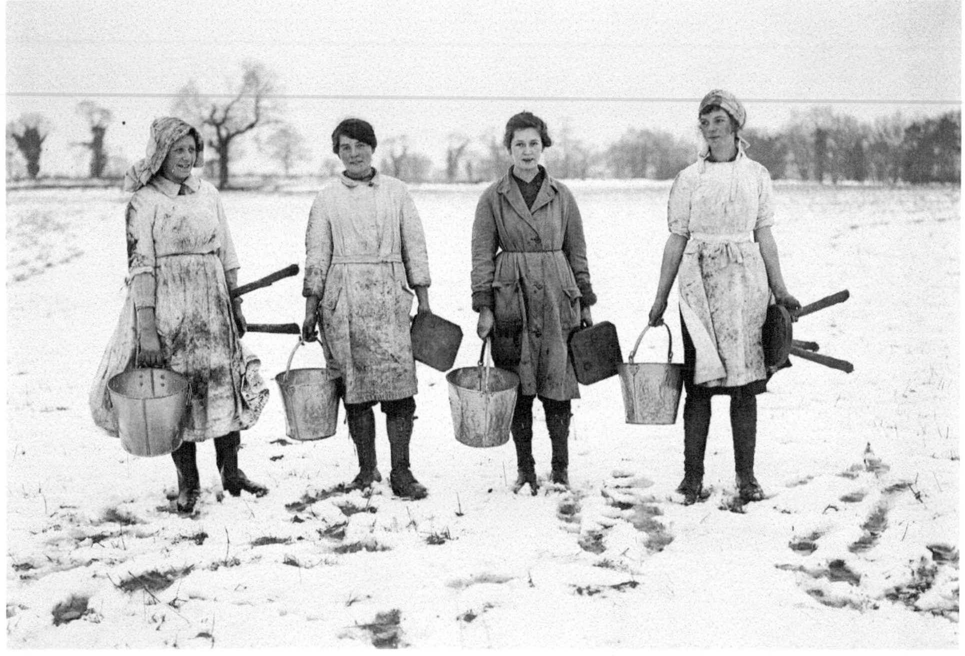

Women's Land Army milkmaids with their milking stools and pails on a cold snowy morning at Thetford, 1918.

buildings. Chamberlins and Harmers undertook considerable work for the manufacture of uniforms under War Office contracts. Norwich was also one of the great boot and shoe manufacturing cities. In the factory of Howlett & White Ltd alone they made 453,000 pairs of boots and shoes for the British Army, 32,000 for the Allies and 21,000 pairs of British Aviation Boots.

It should not be forgotten that Norfolk women had always worked on the land, but in wartime the demands were greater and the likes of the Forage Corps, a branch of the Army Service Corps that consisted mainly of women, harvested and transported fodder from the UK for supply to the front for horses. The Women's Land Army and Women's Forestry Corps were well supported by the women of Norfolk and a hearty number joined the women's branches of all three services when they were created later in the war.

Tanks!

The Brecks in the south of the county made an ideal – and, above all, discreet – area for the first British 'land ships' to be put through their paces in a top-secret training area on Lord Iveagh's estate at Elvedon, near Thetford. To ensure no prying eyes could see, long hoardings covered in hessian were put along the boundaries of the estate near public roads; the excuse for them was that they were there to protect passing traffic from gun shell explosions. When these 'land ships' were finally removed to the front line in 1916

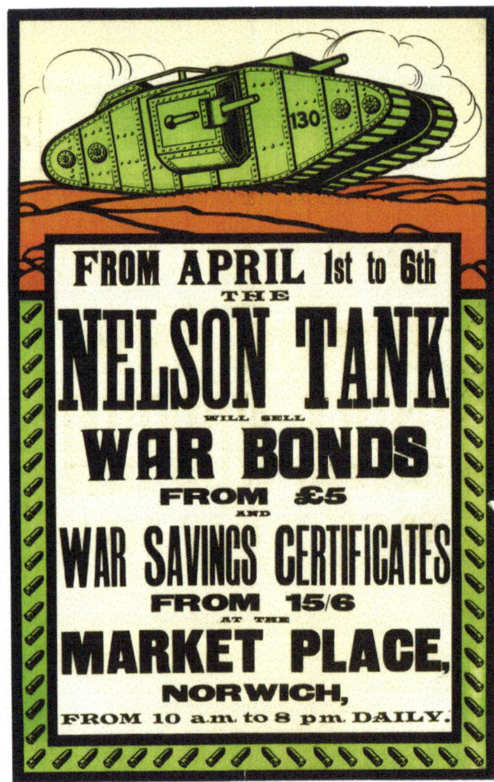

Poster advertising the Norwich Tank Week, April 1918.

their secret was maintained by any reference in their shipment being referred to as 'tanks', as in water tanks. The name stuck.

National War Savings Committee 'Tank Weeks' arranged for a tank to visit cities and large towns around the country to encourage the public to buy War Bonds and War Savings Certificates to raise funds for the war effort. Norwich was visited by Tank 130, *Nelson*, for its Tank Week, which ran from 1–6 April 1918. The city raised well over its £1 million target.

The Generation Passed

Over 12,000 men and women from the county died during or as a direct result of wounds or sickness sustained in the years immediately after the First World War. The last Norfolk Regiment veteran to have served in the First World War who was also a recipient of an Army Long Service and Good Conduct Medal was Frederick John Howlett (1894–1991) of North Walsham. Fred joined as a Kitchener volunteer and proceeded to France with 9th (Service) Battalion, the Norfolk Regiment, in August 1915. After the war he served with 2nd Battalion on the North West Frontier of India.

Henry Allingham, Britain's longest living man, the last serving member of the RNAS and the Royal Air Force from its creation in 1918 was one of our nation's last surviving veterans of the First World War. He served at RNAS stations at Great Yarmouth (where he met his wife to be Dorothy Cator) and Bacton during the conflict. Henry was the last surviving man to have served in uniform in Norfolk during the First World War. He died in 2009 aged 113.

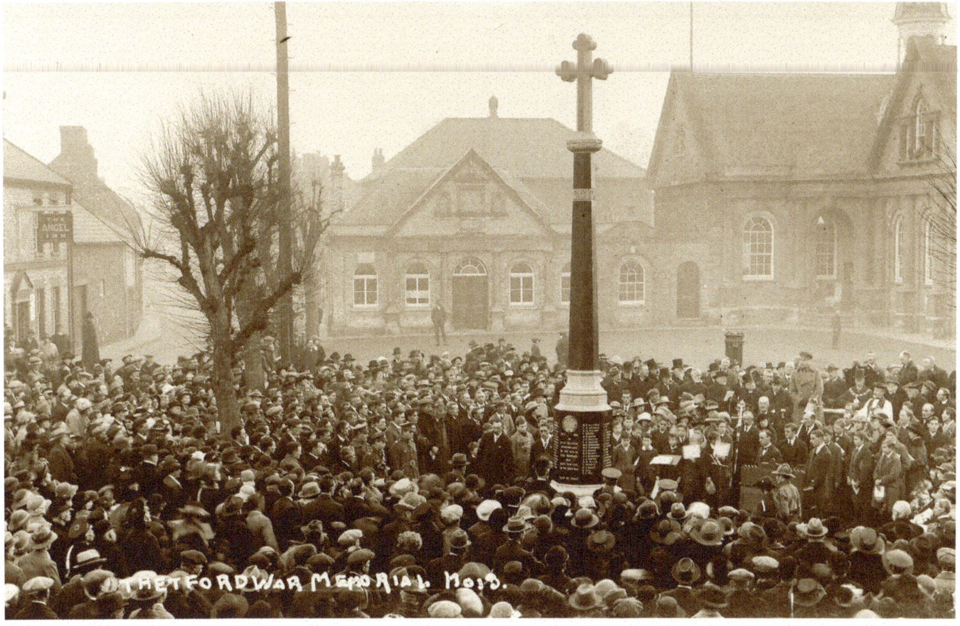

The unveiling of the Thetford War Memorial by Major General Sir Charles Townshend on 4 December 1921. The memorial names 117 men of the town who died during 'The Great War'.

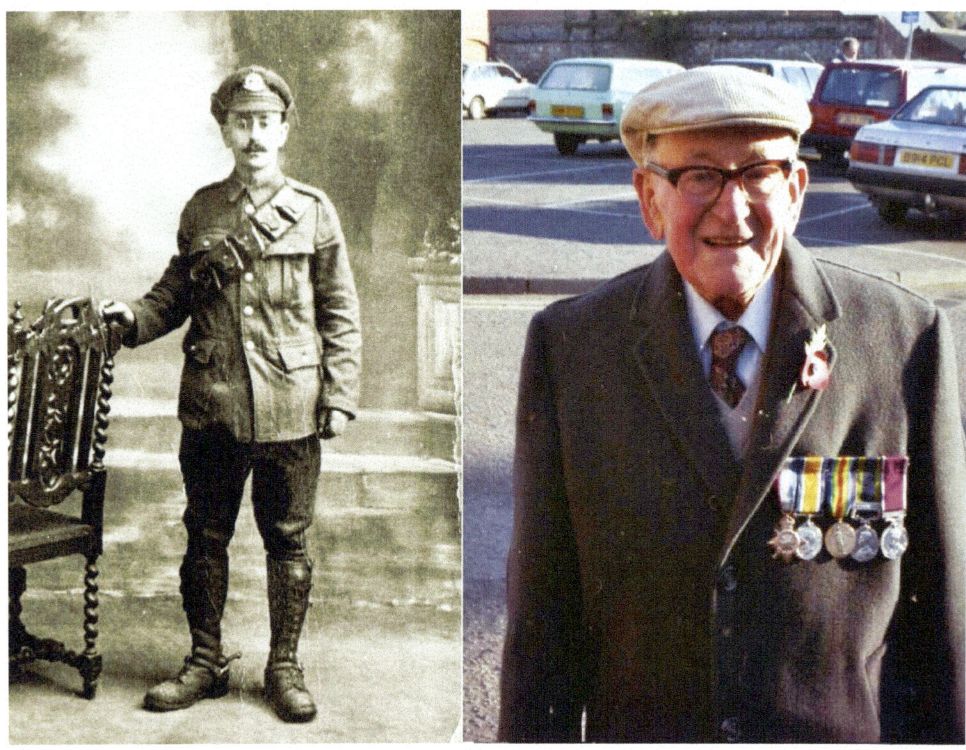

Fred Howlett (1894–1991) of North Walsham, the last veteran of the Norfolk Regiment in receipt of an Army Long Service and Good Conduct Medal to have served in the First World War, pictured during the First World War (left) and at Remembrance Sunday around 1989 (right).

Florence Green (née Patterson) served in the Women's Royal Air Force at RAF Marham and at Narborough airfields in Norfolk during the years 1918–19 and lived to be the world's last surviving veteran of the First World War. Florence lived in King's Lynn for many years and passed away in February 2012 aged 110, the last of that remarkable generation.

8. The Interwar Years

In the years after the First World War the Royal Navy and Royal Air Force kept a presence in the county by continuing to recruit here and maintained a public profile through staging special events and parades. The Army's Territorial Force was disbanded in the immediate aftermath of the First World War. Recruiting began anew in early 1920 and on 1 October 1920 the new Territorial Army was launched. No longer would a TA soldier be asked if he would volunteer for active service abroad if required – it was now part of his obligation as a TA soldier. Changing warfare also meant old yeomanry units had converted to specialist gunnery units either in Anti-Tank (AT) or Anti-Aircraft (AA) roles.

The Norfolk Yeomanry became AT Batteries and land near Carvel Farm Weybourne, after initial use as a summer camp by the AA Division of the TA in 1935, was made a permanent AA training camp in 1937. It was attended by units from across Eastern Command and the London area, and a satellite camp at Stiffkey followed soon after. By the late 1930s the Royal Norfolk Regiment and Norfolk Yeomanry TA units were joined

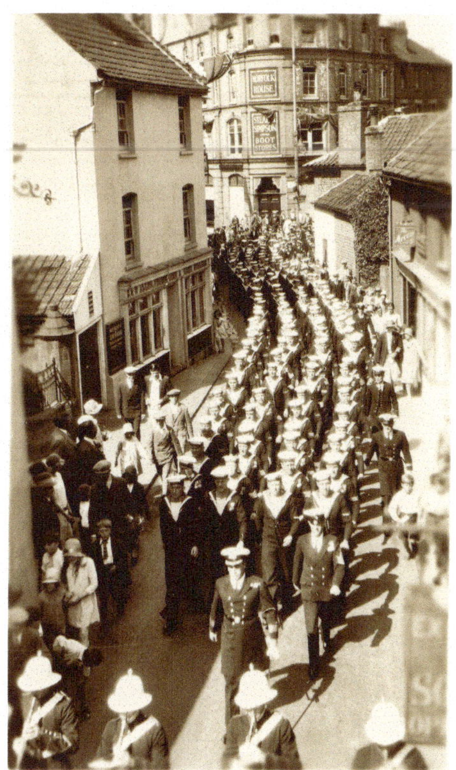

Ship's Company parade through Cromer led by a Royal Marines band. Parades, tattoos and pageants were a regular feature of armed forces life during the interwar years.

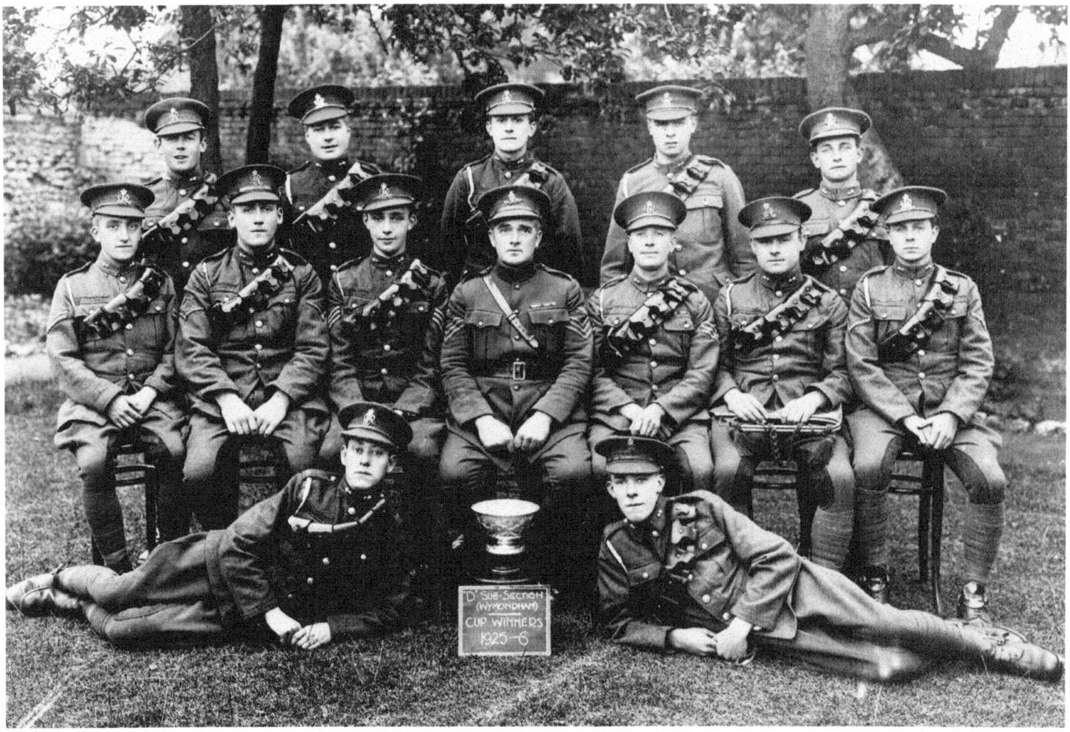

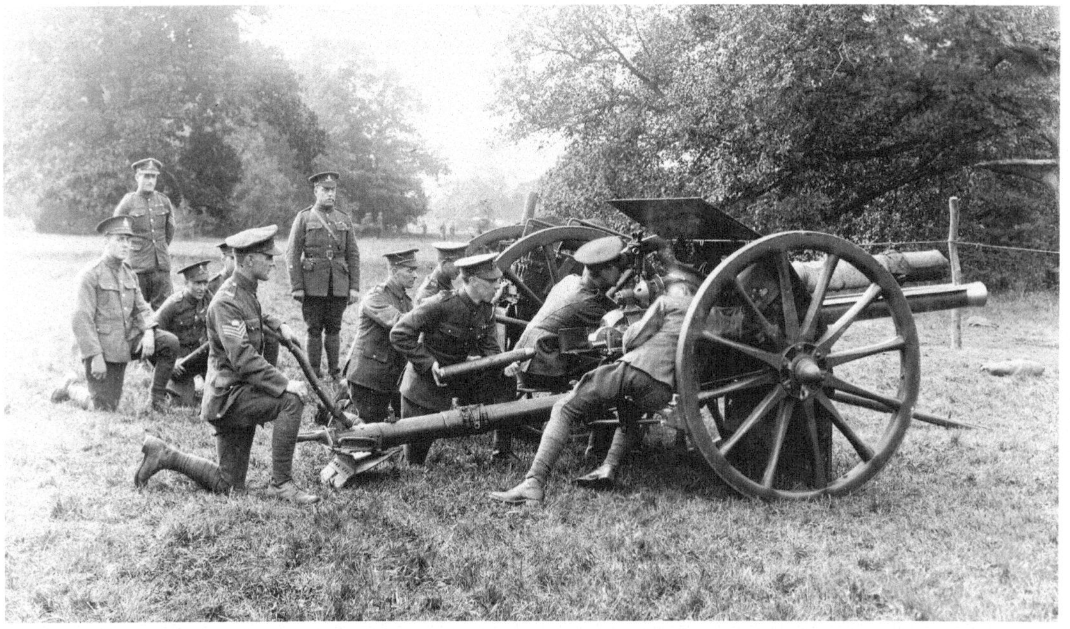

'D' Sub-Section (Wymondham), Norfolk Yeomanry, cup winners 1925–26.

Men of the Norfolk Yeomanry practising gun drill under the watchful eye of the Battery Sergeant Major, *c.* 1925.

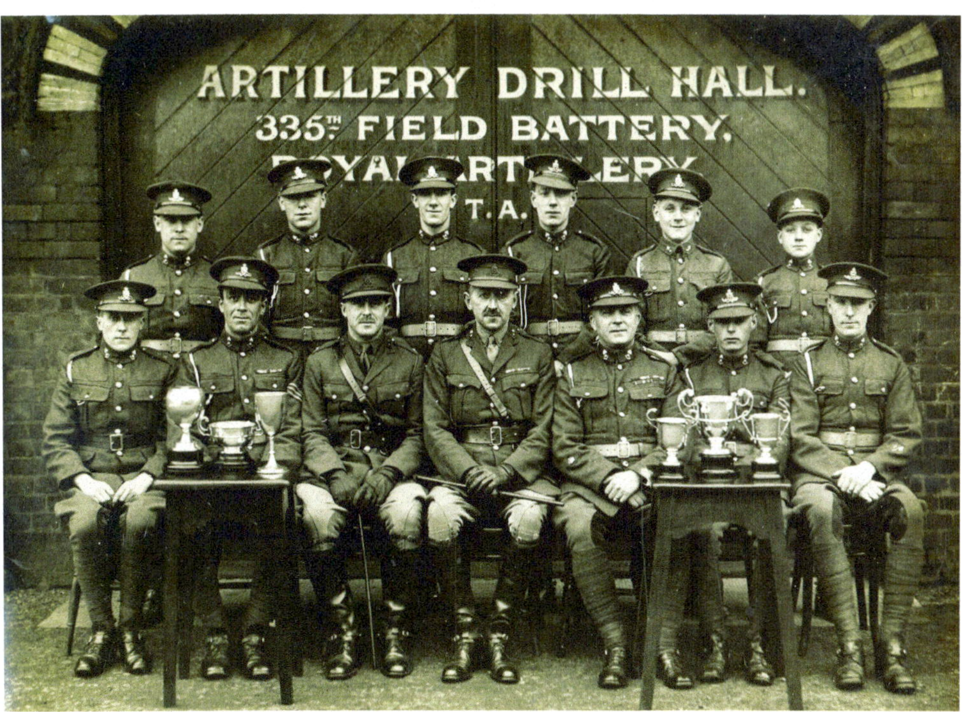

Above: The prize-winning competition team, BSM and officers of 335 Field Battery, Royal Field Artillery (TA) outside the Artillery Drill Hall, Great Yarmouth, in the 1920s.

Right: Recruiting leaflet for the raising of a new Battery of the Norfolk Yeomanry at King's Lynn, May 1939.

THE NORFOLK YEOMANRY.

(55th. S. & N. Yeo. A T. Rgt. R.A. T.A.)

Recruits of good education are required for

A NEW BATTERY

Of this Regiment, to be raised at King's Lynn

A RECRUITING MEETING

to be held at the Town Hall, King's Lynn, on MONDAY, MAY 1st, 1939, at 8 p.m.

ALL ARE WELCOME.

The Battery is armed with—ANTI-TANK GUNS,
BREN GUNS,
ANTI-TANK RIFLES.

IT IS A COMPLETELY MECHANIZED UNIT.

CONDITIONS OF SERVICE (Ages 17—38).

Engagements—4 years (with extensions).

Training Period—Nov.-May, during which a minimum of 45 hours for 1st year and of 20 hours in succeeding years is required to qualify for Annual Bounty.

Annual Camp—14 days, held outside the County.

Pay—Regular Army Rates at Camp. Marriage Allowance at Camp. Bounty (as above) if qualified.

Applications to Mr. P. Heywood,

Messrs. A. & J. Bowker, opposite Town Hall

JOIN NOW !

AND MAKE IT A "KING'S LYNN" BATTERY OF YOUR FRIENDS.

J. A. Gould, Printer, Swaffham.

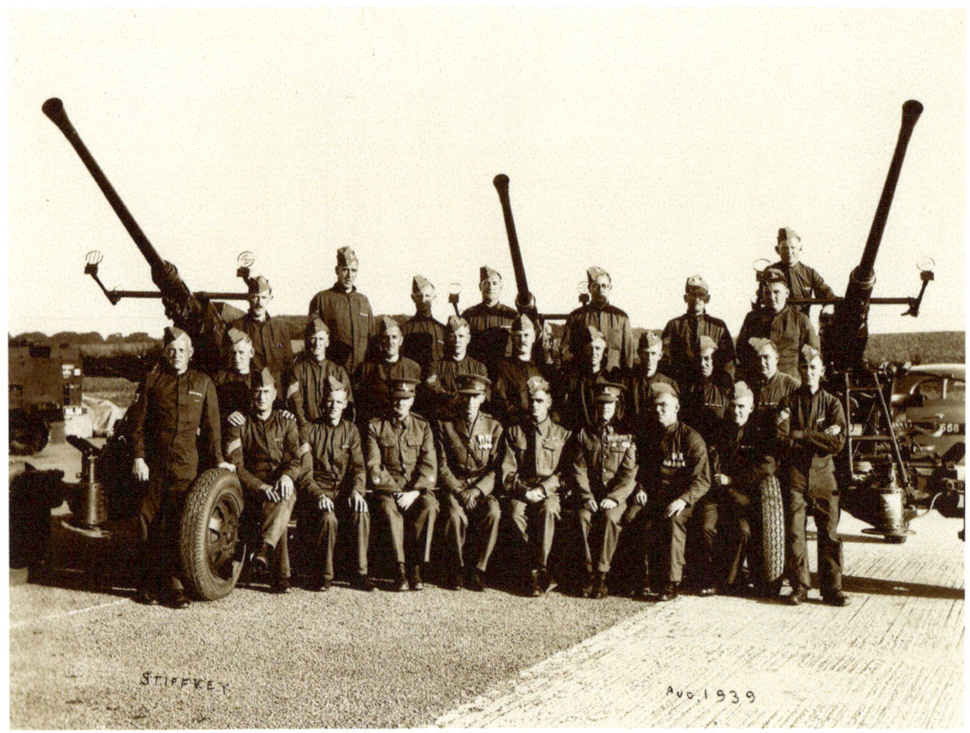

Anti-aircraft gunners and their Bofors guns at Stiffkey Artillery Camp, August 1939.

in Norwich by 250th Company, Royal Engineers, 183rd (East Anglian) Field Ambulance and Workshop Company, 41st AA Divisional Royal Army Ordnance Corps. The newest recruiting centre in the city, for the Royal Air Force Volunteer Reserve, opened in July 1939; however, after the outbreak of war the large number of volunteers swamped the extant recruiting offices, so a combined Royal Navy, Army and RAF recruiting centre was opened shortly after the outbreak of war at the Norwich Agricultural Hall.

9. The Second World War

War was declared on 3 September 1939 and within days the natural harbours, beaches and quays of Norfolk were assessed by the War Office for their viability as troop landing areas amid fears of invasion. The conflict at first seemed very distant, even a 'phoney war', that is until May 1940 when the situation declined in France. Britain's defences were then addressed in earnest as we faced a direct threat of invasion. The number of emergency gun batteries along the coast were increased and all manner of pill boxes, anti-tank obstacles and fixed defences were strung out along the coastline, inland stop lines and vulnerable points. The landing of enemy troops by seaplanes on the Broads was also feared, so motorboats were acquired by the military, patrols were organised and a number of the Broads were laid with underwater mines.

The Great Yarmouth Royal Navy base HMS *Watchful* protected shipping convoys with its flotilla of motor torpedo boats, salvage tugs and air-sea rescue boats. In 1940 HMS *Miranda* was established as a dedicated base for the minesweeping trawlers at the Fishwharf and

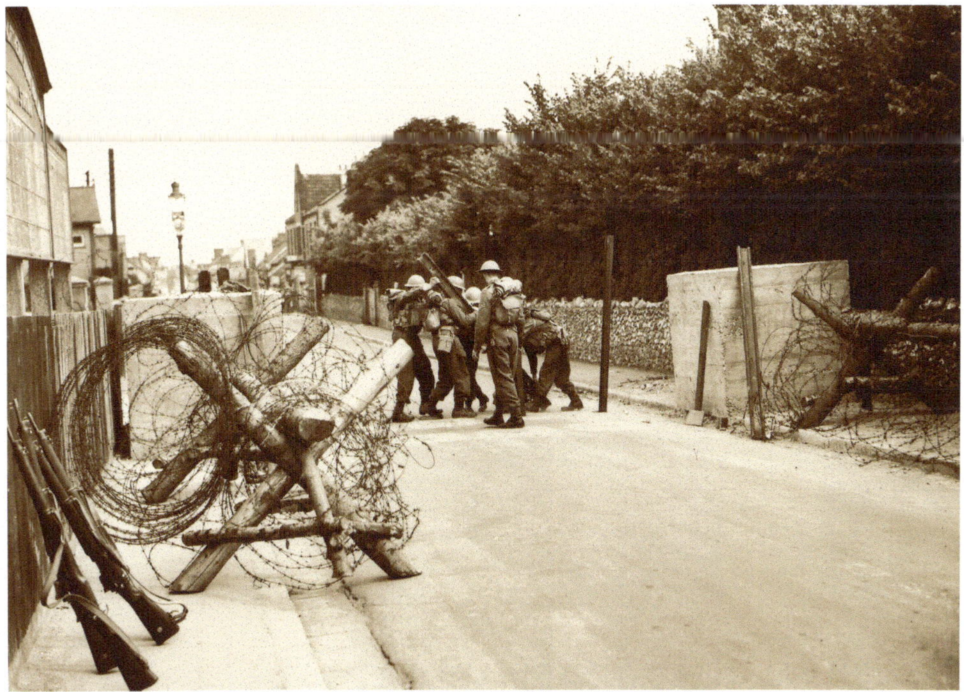

Soldiers of 6th Battalion, the Royal Norfolk Regiment (TA) assembling roadblock defences between the anti-tank blocks at the top of Station Road, Sheringham, 1940.

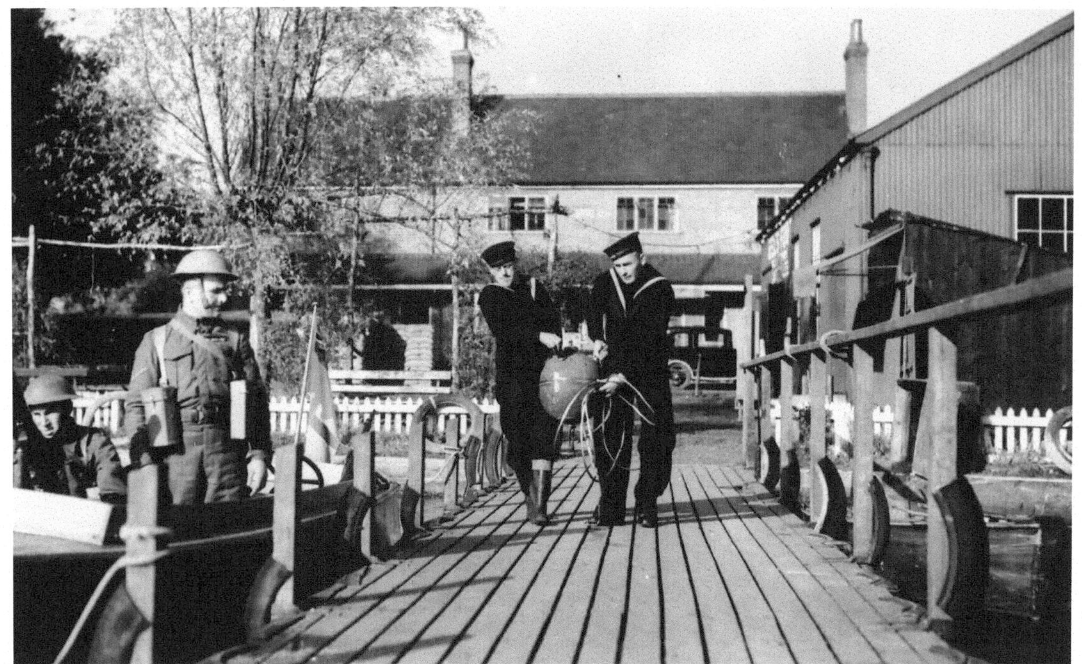

Sailors manhandling a mine to one of the boats of the Broads Flotilla at the Ormesby Broad sub-base, the Eels Foot, Ormesby, August 1940.

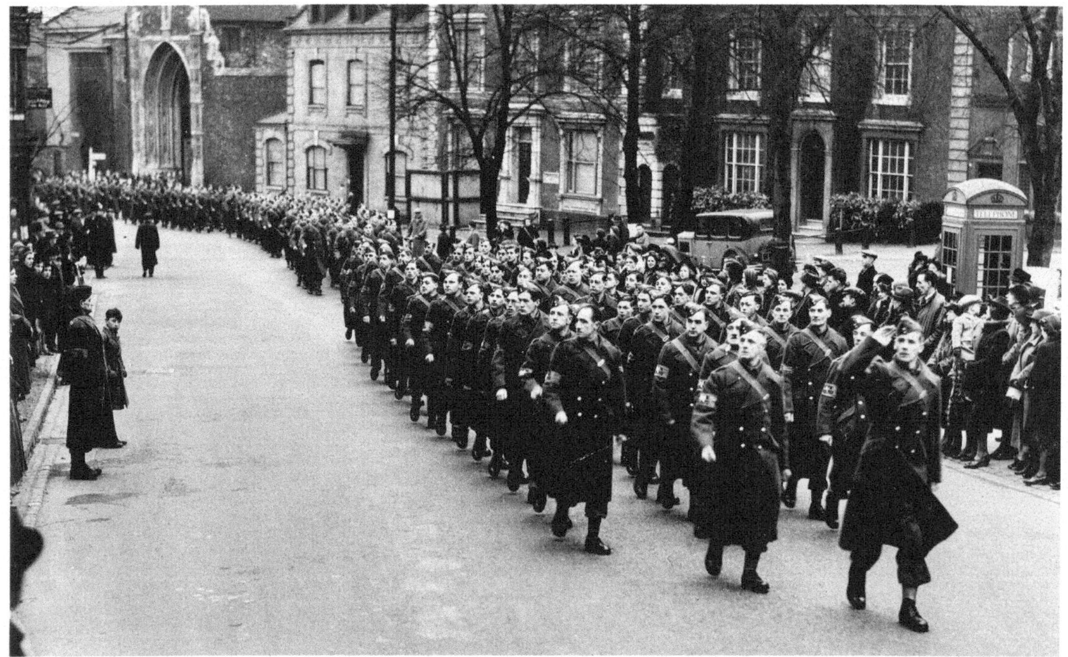

The Signals Company of Norwich Home Guard (note their crossed flags over their armbands) with eyes right as they march up Tombland after a service at the cathedral, 1940.

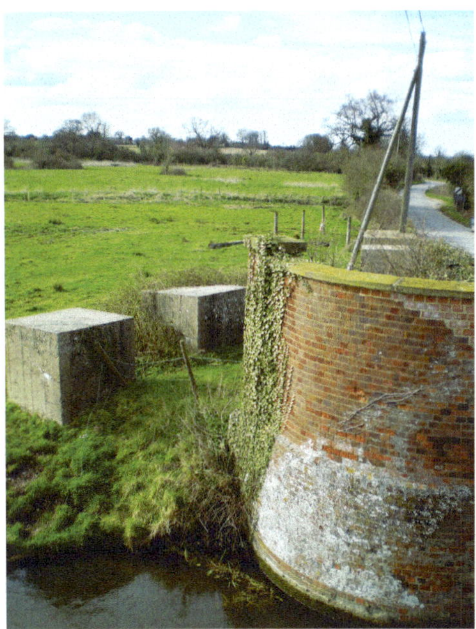 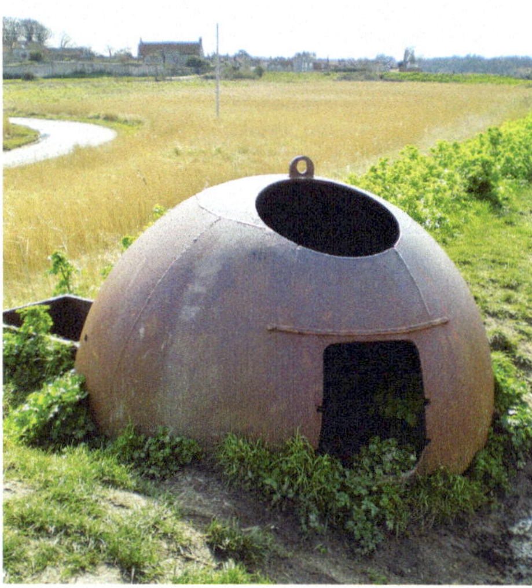

Above left: Anti-invasion defence anti-tank blocks dating from 1940 near the river bridge at Burgh-next-Aylsham.

Above right: An Alan Williams Turret at Cley. Installed in 1940, the turret was ideal for both beach defence and for defending vulnerable positions. It could be manned by two men, could rotate 360 degrees, had a hatch on top for anti-aircraft firing and could be used to fire machine guns or even the Boys Anti-Tank Rifle.

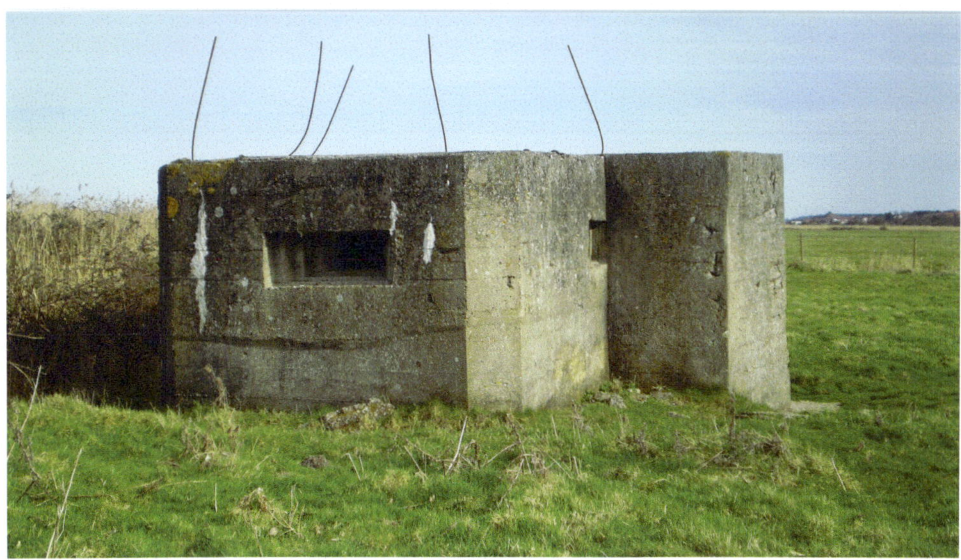

Composite pillbox at Holkham consisting of two Vickers Machine Gun emplacements set together at an angle to give field of fire from the main embrasures at 90 degrees to each other.

was joined from January 1941 by HMS *Midge* as Yarmouth's coastal forces base with specific responsibility for motor torpedo boats, motor gun boats and mine layers.

Fears of invasion led to an appeal for Local Defence Volunteers in May 1940, which ultimately resulted in the creation of seventeen Home Guard battalions in the county who stood ready to defend their homes from paratroops or invaders. Thousands of local men and women served in the armed services all over the world during the war. There were certainly pre-war regular soldiers and local Territorials who were mobilised. There were also plenty of those who volunteered, but there were also many did not have any choice and were conscripted from 1939.

Air Raids

In anticipation of enemy air raids there were a number of RAF bases in the county to intercept the enemy in the air. Fixed and mobile anti-aircraft guns and searchlights were deployed along the coast at strategic points around the county and around Norwich. There was also an extensive Air Raid Precautions (ARP) scheme of wardens, rescue parties, aid posts, ambulance crews and welfare workers. Enemy aircraft were on mine-laying missions off the coast during the winter of 1939. The first bombs fell on the county shortly after midnight on 25 May 1940, when thirteen high-explosive (HE) bombs were dropped to the north-east of RAF West Raynham.

Norwich suffered its first air raid on 9 July 1940. Bombs were dropped on Barnards Factory on Salhouse Road, Mousehold, Thorpe railway station, Boulton and Paul's Riverside Works, and on Carrow Hill just as the workers were leaving after 'knocking off' time. A number of men and women were killed during the raid and many others were wounded, with some suffering injuries that later proved fatal.

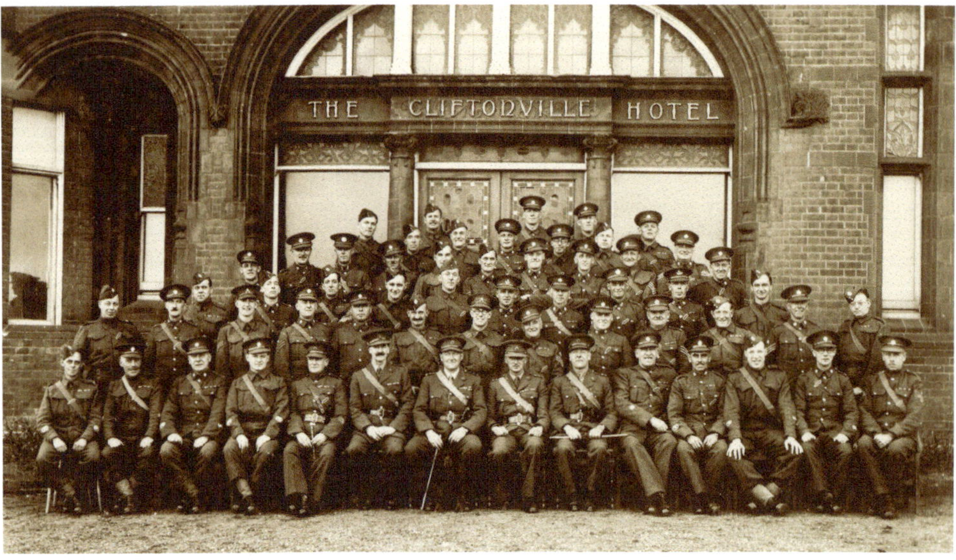

Staff of No. 10 Driving Training Centre, Royal Army Service Corps staff, based at the Cliftonville Hotel, Cromer, 1940.

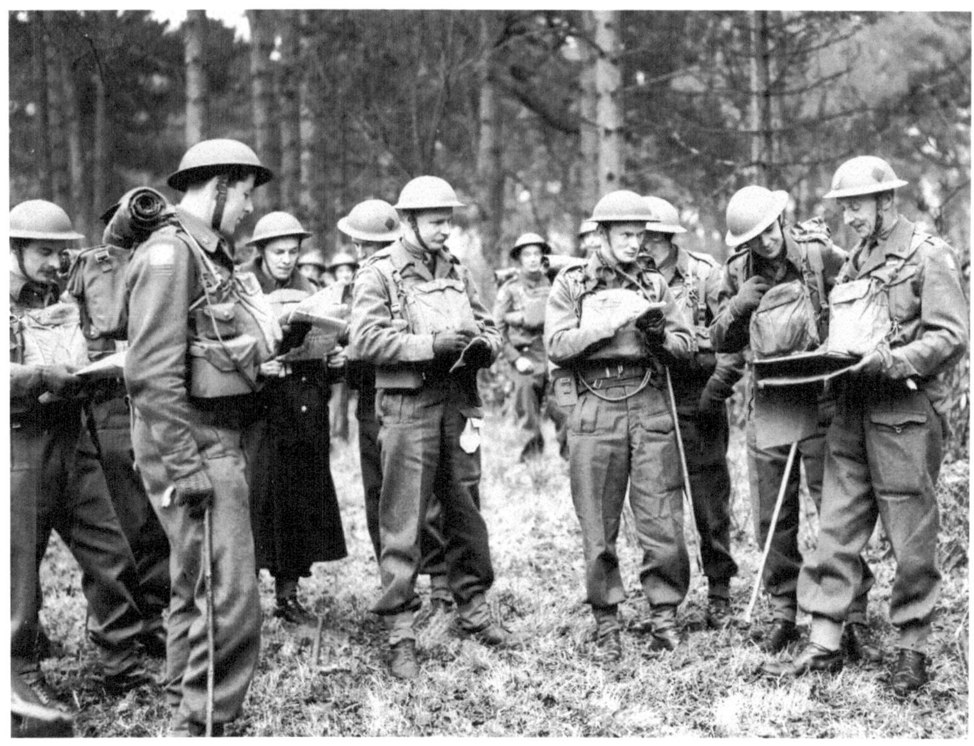

Officers of 2/5th Battalion, Sherwood Foresters, 139 Brigade, 46th Division, gather for a briefing before setting out on manoeuvres near Norwich, 1941.

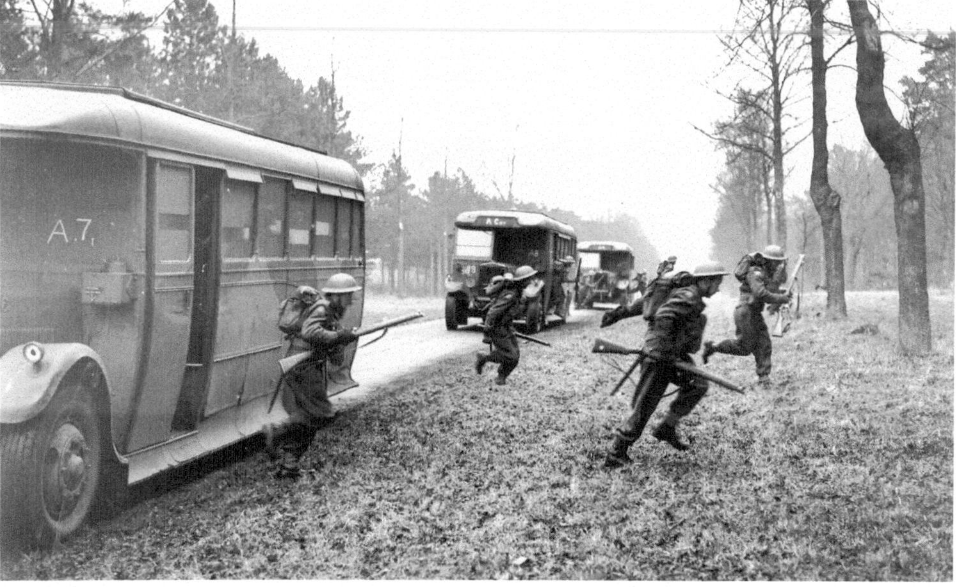

Rapid deployment of troops from requisitioned buses painted with camouflage paint during 46th Division manoeuvres near Norwich 1941.

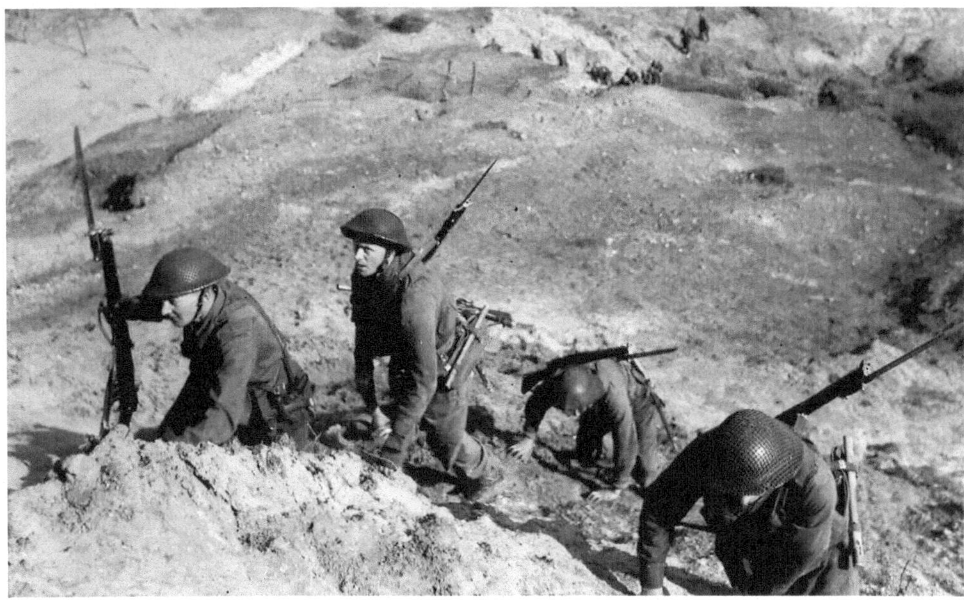

Soldiers of 1st Battalion, the Duke of Wellington's Regiment practice a beach landing and cliff assault with live machine gun and mortar fire at Cromer, April 1942.

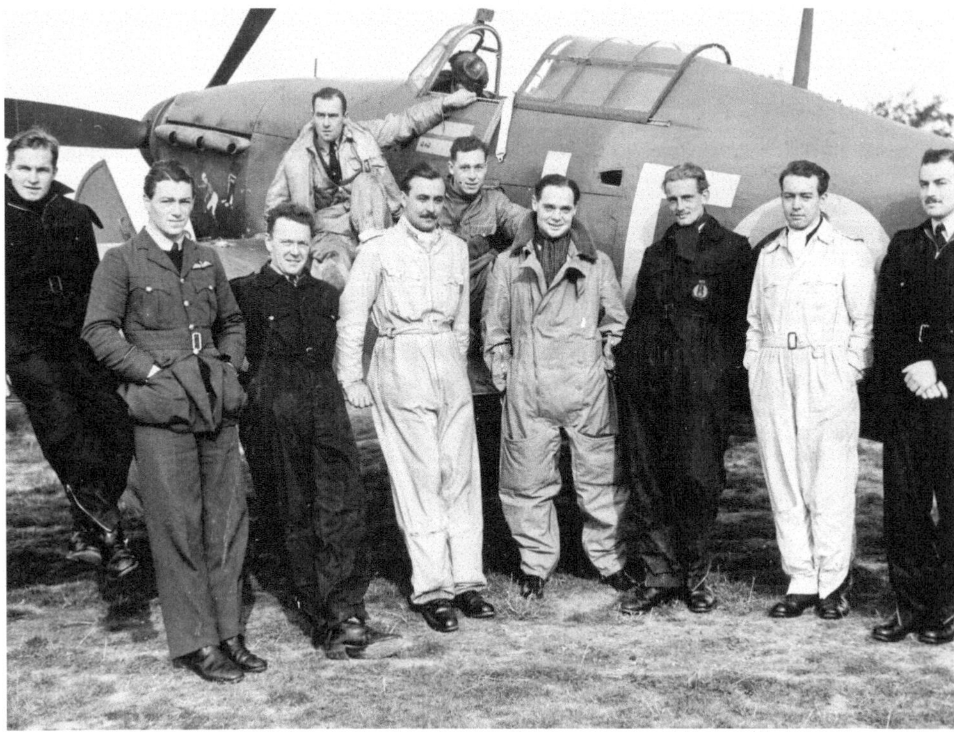

Pilots of 242 Squadron, RAF Coltishall, during the Battle of Britain 1940. In the centre of the photograph with his hands in his pockets is Squadron Leader Douglas Bader.

Great Yarmouth suffered its worst year of bombing in 1941. A total of 767 alerts were sounded and 1,328 'crash' warnings given. A total of 167 raids were conducted on the town, during which 803 high-explosive bombs and six mines exploded in the borough destroying many of the old 'Rows'. An estimated 7,020 incendiary bombs rained down and fifty-five UXBs had to be dealt with by bomb-disposal squads. Over 100 people lost their lives, 329 were injured and the historic townscape of Great Yarmouth was changed forever.

After the failure of the bombing campaigns to destroy either the airfields or London, Hitler planned to break British morale by attempting to destroy the country's picturesque and historic places, selecting those marked with three stars in the German *Baedeker's Guide to Great Britain*. On the nights of 27–28 and 29–30 April 1942 Norwich received its heaviest raids of the war when 90 tons of bombs were dropped on the city, claiming sixty-seven lives. It was also in 1942 that King's Lynn suffered its worst loss of life when the Eagle Hotel on Norfolk Street received a direct hit, killing forty-two people during a raid on 12 June 1942.

The coastal areas of the county were also subjected to 'tip and run' air raids, where enemy bombers would make landfall and rapidly drop their bombs. On 11 May 1943 twenty Focke-Wulf 190s appeared over Great Yarmouth at 8.45 a.m. as a platoon of thirty ATS women were marching back to their billet at Sefton House on the seafront. The raiders screamed towards them, one of them opened up with his machine guns and as the ATS ran into their hostel for cover one of the raiders dropped a bomb on the building. A total of twenty-six girls lost their lives, an incident described as the largest single military loss of British servicewomen. Twenty-three civilians, mostly mothers and children, were also killed and forty-one injured by the other bombs that fell on the town in the same raid.

In Norwich over 30,000 houses were damaged – 2,000 of them beyond repair – and 340 people were killed as a result of air raids on the city during the Second World War.

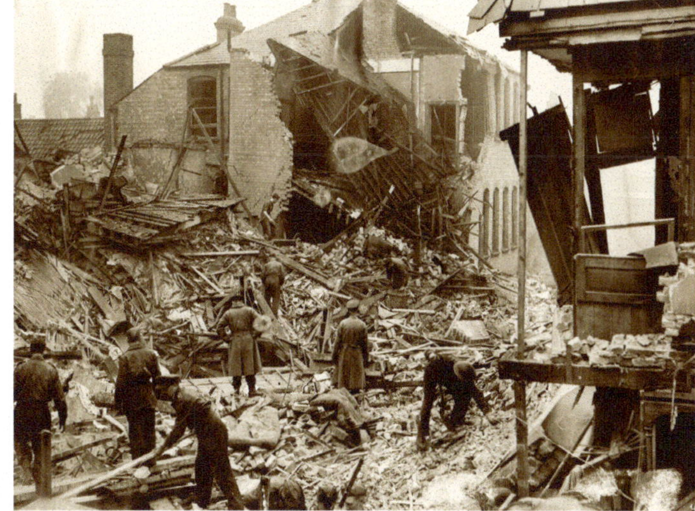

Rescue workers searching the wreckage of the Eagle Hotel, King's Lynn, after the town had suffered its worst raid on 12 June 1942, where forty-two local people and service personnel were killed.

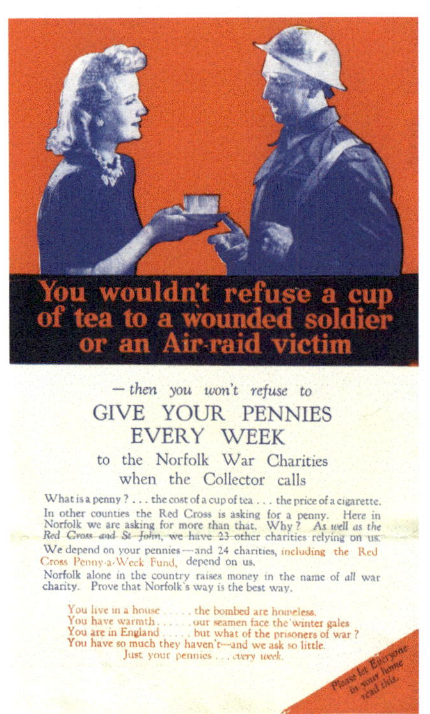

Left: Leaflet for the Norfolk War Charities Penny-a-Week Fund. Started in 1940 to co-ordinate appeals on behalf of over thirty charities in the county, when the fund closed in 1945, it had raised half a million pounds.

Below: The Royal Navy contingent march past Norwich City Hall on the Norwich 'Wings For Victory' parade 1943.

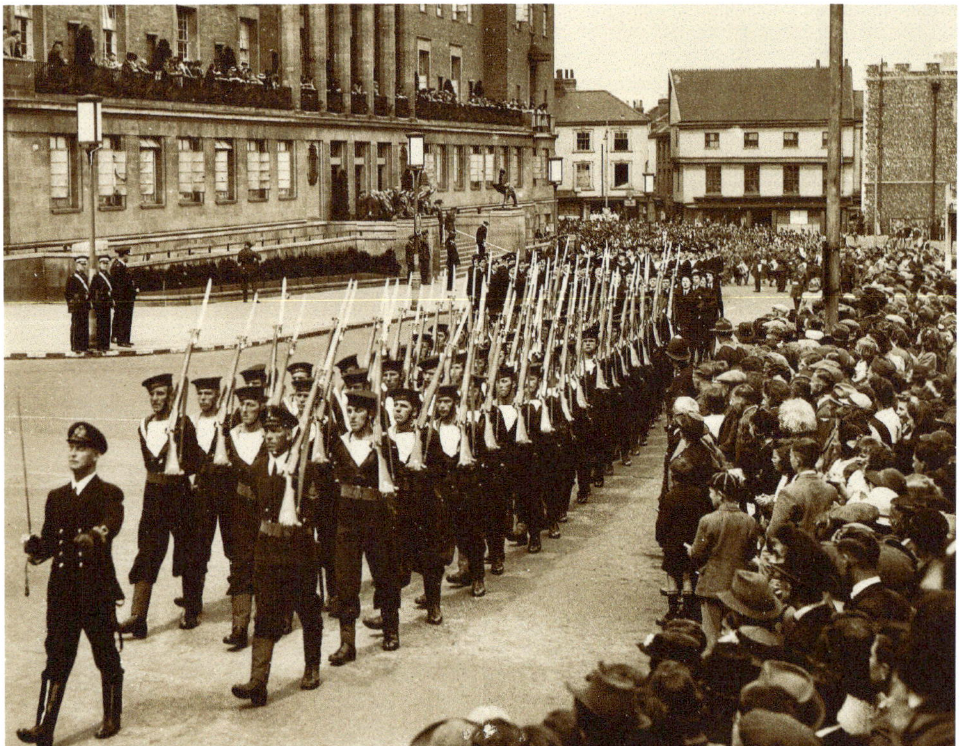

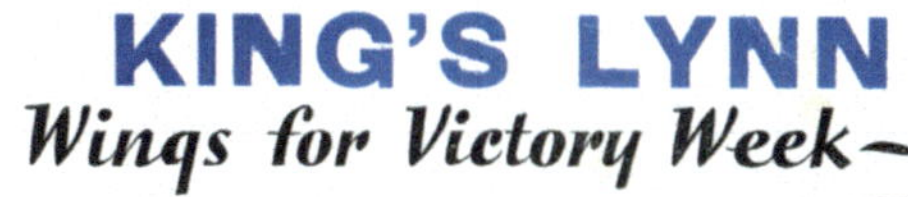

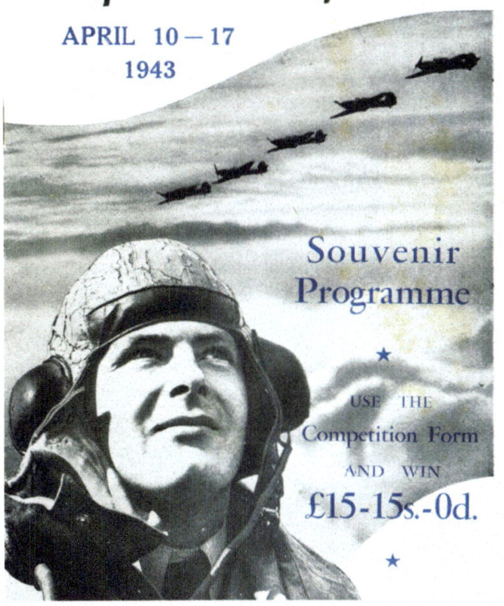

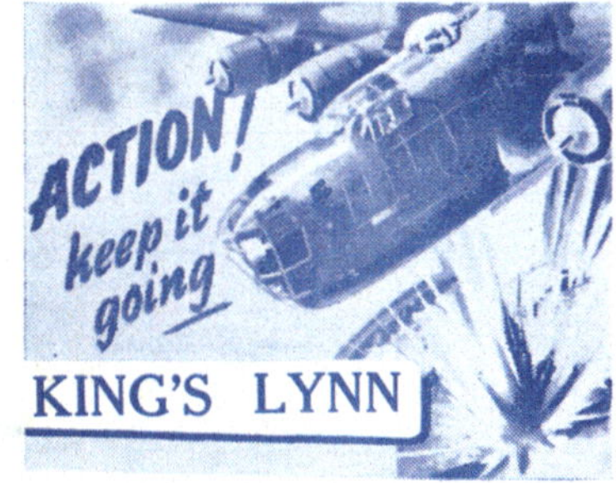

Souvenir programme for the King's Lynn 'Wings for Victory' week, April 1943.

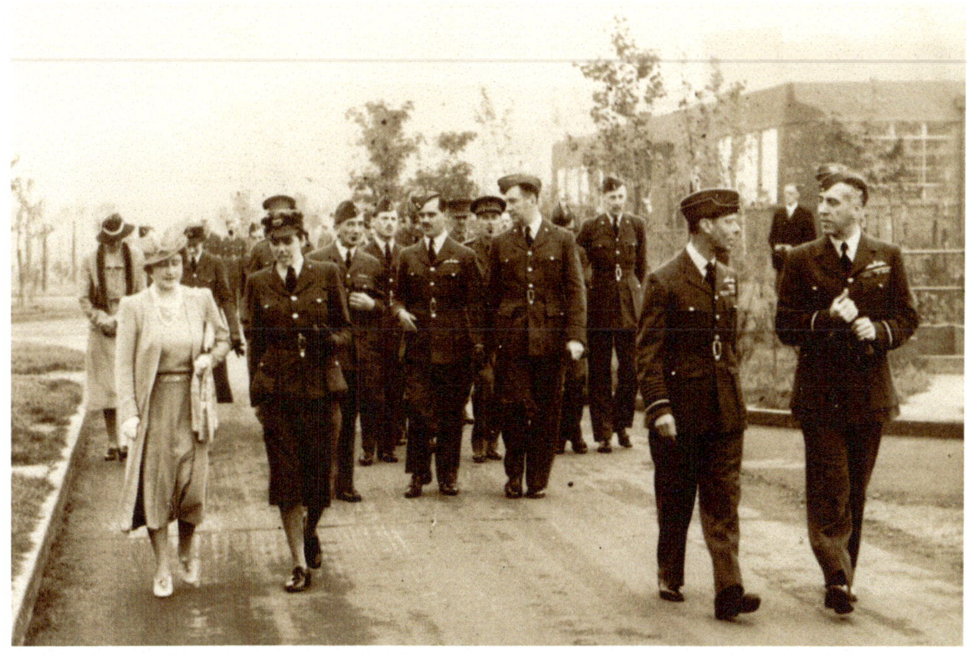

George V and Queen Elizabeth during an official visit to visit RAF West Raynham, *c.* 1943.

The Friendly Invasion

The first American B17 bombers and P38 fighters and crews arrived in Britain in July 1942, and by mid-1944 the Eighth Air Force had grown to become the biggest military air fleet ever seen, with 122 bases, 200,000 personnel, 2,000 four engine bombers and 1,000 fighter aircraft and entered into history as the 'Mighty Eighth'. Two American Air Divisions had bases in Norfolk, with a total of eighteen USAAF airfields across the county. The 2nd Air Division had the largest presence in the county, predominantly flying Consolidated B-24 Liberators. The first USAAF heavy-bomber base in Norfolk was opened at Shipdam in October 1942.

A number of airfields under construction for RAF bombers – such as Tibenham, Snetterton Heath and Wendling – were rescheduled for USAAF use and an unprecedented programme of new-build airfields rolled out across the county. Extant RAF bases such as Horsham St Faith, East Wretham or Watton were also occupied by the USAAF. Once completed, each airfield was occupied by a single Bombardment Group consisting of four flying Bombardment Squadrons – a squadron had an average compliment of twelve to sixteen bombers with 200 combat airmen. The total personnel on a bomber station varied between 2,000 and 3,000. The sudden arrival of thousands of service personnel from the USA in the Eastern Counties was known as 'the Friendly Invasion' and their bases as the 'Fields of Little America'. Some 6,700 men of the 2nd Air Division USAAF were killed in action flying from local air fields during the war.

V-2 Rocket Attacks

The V-2 was a long-range rocket known in Germany as the *Vergeltungswaffe 2* – a retaliation weapon. While London was the main target, 'short falls' of 'V' weapons could

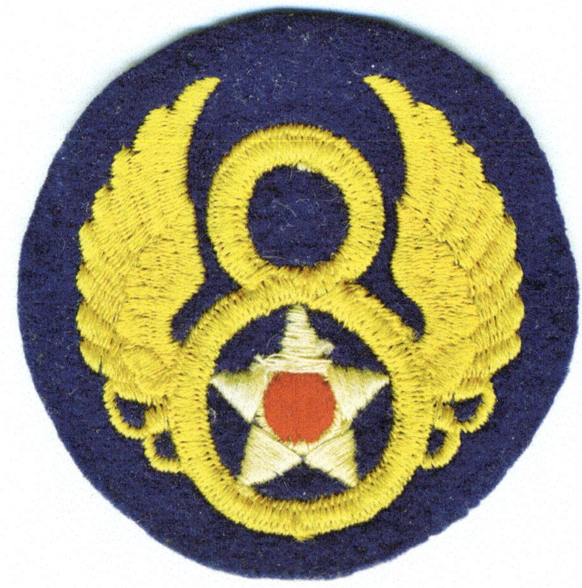

Sleeve badge worn on the uniforms of the 'Mighty Eighth' United States Army Air Force that had numerous bases in the county in 1942–45.

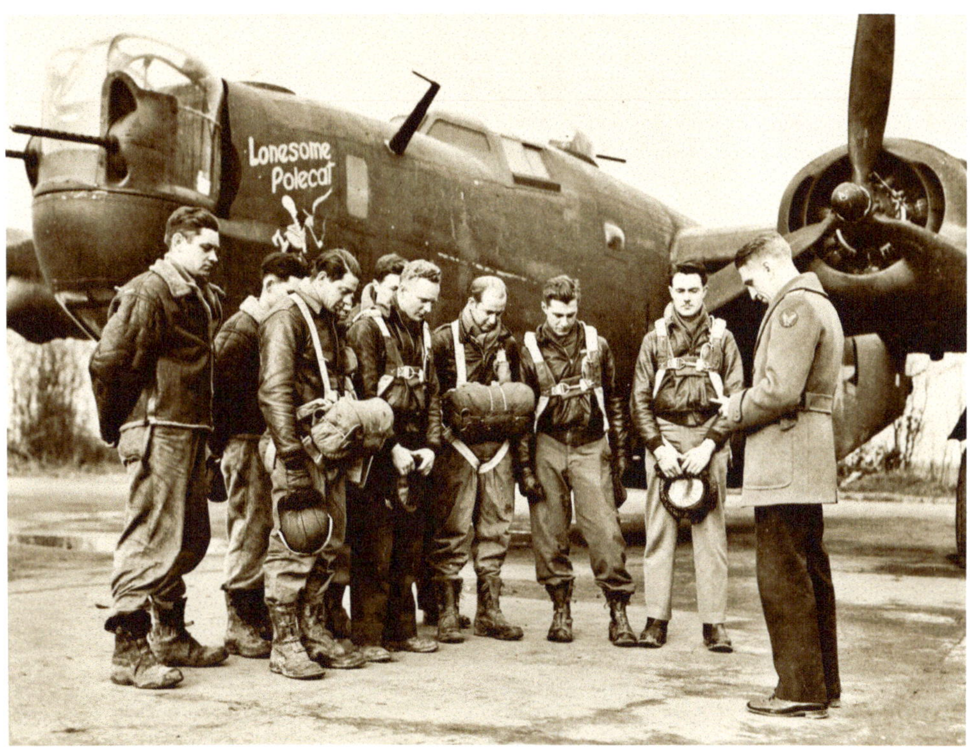

Above: Captain James A. Burrsi, Chaplain, leads ground and flight crews of the B-24 Liberator '*The Lonesome Polecat*' 577nd Bomb Squadron, 392nd Bomb Group, 8th USAAF in prayer before they take off on a mission from their airfield at Wendling. 'Lonesome Polecat' is believed to have been shot down by German fighters near Peenemunde and crashed into the Baltic with the loss of all crew on 9 April 1944.

Right: Major James 'Jimmy' Stewart was an accomplished pre-war pilot and flew numerous missions with 445th BG out of Tibbenham and 453rd BG at Old Buckenham during the war.

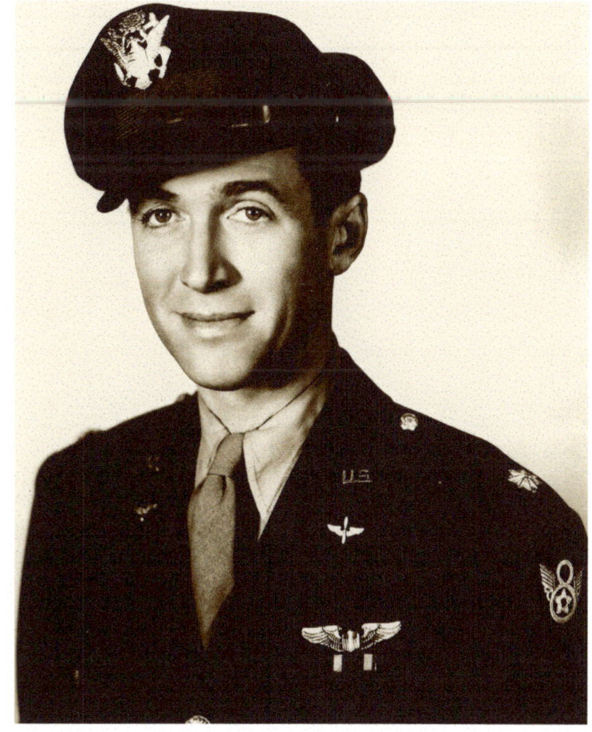

occur over much of south-east England, and there were also other targets, including the city of Norwich. Operated by Versuchs Artillerie Batterie 444, the launch site for the attacks on the city was in a wood near Rijs in south-west Friesland, Holland.

The first V-2 that fell on Norfolk crashed into a field near Ranworth on 26 September 1944, which caused a great explosion and crater and sent a column of smoke 2,000 feet in the air. Norwich was never hit by a V-2; the nearest crashed on the golf course at Hellesdon on 3 October 1944 causing minor damage to some 400 homes in the area between Dereham Road and Boundary Road. The only casualty was an elderly lady who was treated for shock. More rockets would follow, but by some miracle no one was killed in any of the V-2 landings on the county. The very last V-2 to fall on Norfolk crashed at Welborne, near Mattishall, on 26 October 1944.

VE Day and VJ Day 1945

After the success of the Normandy landings and successful advances into north-western Europe the Home Guard were stood down in the last months of 1944. Victory in Europe in May and Victory over Japan in September 1945 heralded the end of the Second World War. There were great celebrations, but just like the First World War, not too many years before, they were tinged with sadness. While many families were reunited with loved ones who had returned from the services, there were also many families who never saw their loved ones again.

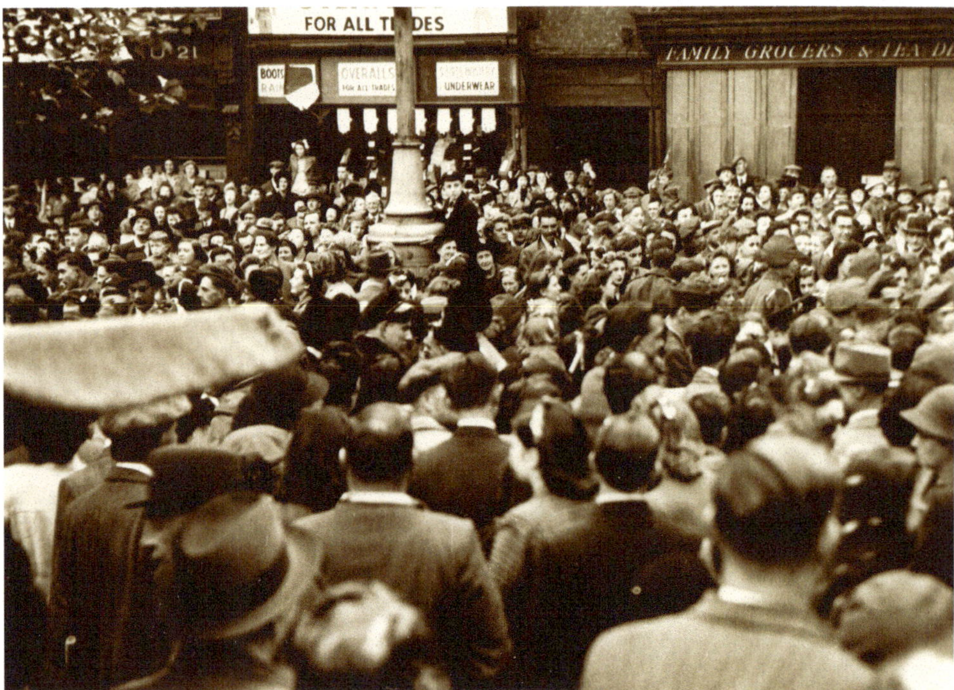

Crowds throng Norwich Market Place and Gentleman's Walk, Norwich, to celebrate VE Day, 8 May 1945.

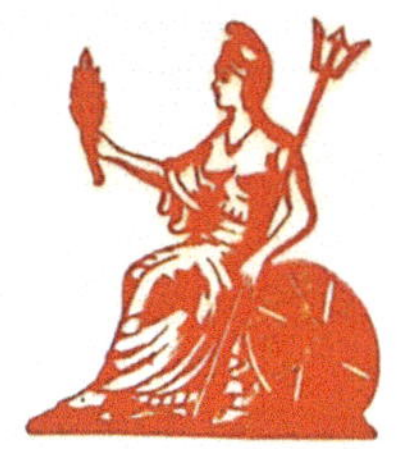

6th Bn. Norfolk Home Guard

Commanded by Lt.-Col. A. R. Taylor

❋

FINAL PARADE

HELD AT

Britannia Barracks, Norwich
On Sunday, Nov. 26th, 1944

❋

INSPECTION BY

FIELD-MARSHAL LORD IRONSIDE
G.C.B., C.M.G., D.S.O.

accompanied by

COL. A. C. PARRY, M.B.E., M.C.
and
COL. B. M. EDWARDS, M.C., D.L., J.P.

·

DIVINE SERVICE
conducted by Rev. W. M. Lummis, M.C.

·

MARCH - PAST
led by the Band of the Suffolk Regiment

Cover of the service sheet for the stand-down parade of 6th Battalion, Norfolk Home Guard, 26 November 1944.

10. The Royal Norfolk Regiment

The Royal Norfolk Regiment was the senior of all East Anglian regiments. Originally raised during the Monmouth Rebellion in 1685 as Colonel Henry Cornwall's Regiment, their unique regimental badge – that of Britannia – was bestowed upon the regiment by Queen Anne in recognition of their bravery and steadfastness at the Battle of Almanza in 1707. The regiment was designated the 9th Regiment of Foot in 1751 and would often be simply referred to as 'the Ninth' for many years afterwards. The original regimental march was *Young May Moon*, until 1880 when *Rule Britannia* by Dr Thomas Augustine Arne was adopted.

The Ninth fought in the American War of Independence but were surrendered with General Burgoyne at the Battle of Saratoga in 1777. Concerned the colours of the regiment would fall into the hands of the enemy, they were removed from their poles by Lieutenant Colonel Hill and secreted in his baggage trunks throughout their period of captivity. On the return of the regiment to Britain in 1781, the colours were presented to the king and were deposited for display at Sandhurst. The 'Saratoga Colours' remain the oldest surviving colours in the British Army. In 1782 it was decreed that each regiment should no longer just be known as a number, but should also bear the names of a county to build

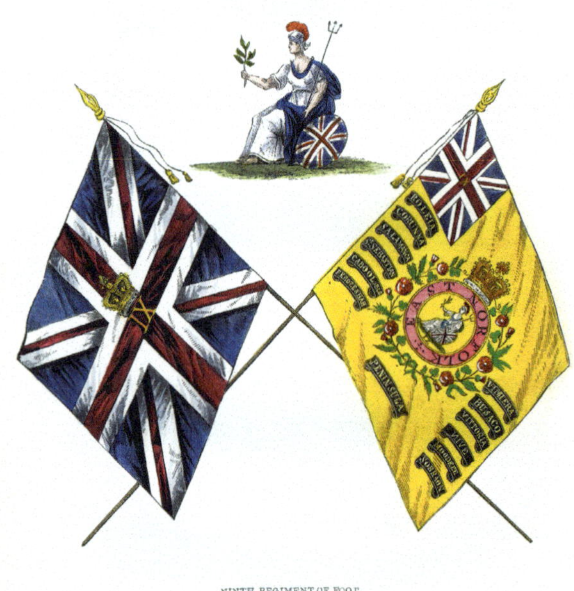

The figure of Britannia badge and colours of the 9th (East Norfolk) Regiment, *c.* 1850.

a mutual attachment, which would be useful towards recruitment for the regiment – thus the Ninth adopted the appellation 'the East Norfolk Regiment'.

The 'Holy Boys'

The Ninth fought in Spain and Portugal during the Peninsular Campaign of the Napoleonic Wars. Contrary to some stories that tell of our soldiers selling Bibles for beer, the nickname of 'the Holy Boys' came about because the figure of Britannia – emblazoned upon the regimental colour and badges – was mistaken by locals in the Catholic counties for the Virgin Mary, as such the entire regiment were believed to be made up of 'holy men'.

During the Peninsular War the Ninth provided the rearguard for the evacuation of the beach during the Battle of Corunna on 16 January 1809. Their final act before leaving was to bury the body of their divisional commander, Sir John Moore. Ever since that time black details have featured on the uniform of the regiments in memory of Sir John and the battle honour of Corunna. Other significant engagements during the campaign were emblazoned on the colours of the regiment.

Soldiers of the Queen and the King

Battalions of the regiment were almost continually serving out in India and the Middle East from the mid-nineteenth century – both on active service and garrison duty. In one remarkable feat of soldiering during the First Sikh War, the regiment marched 150 miles

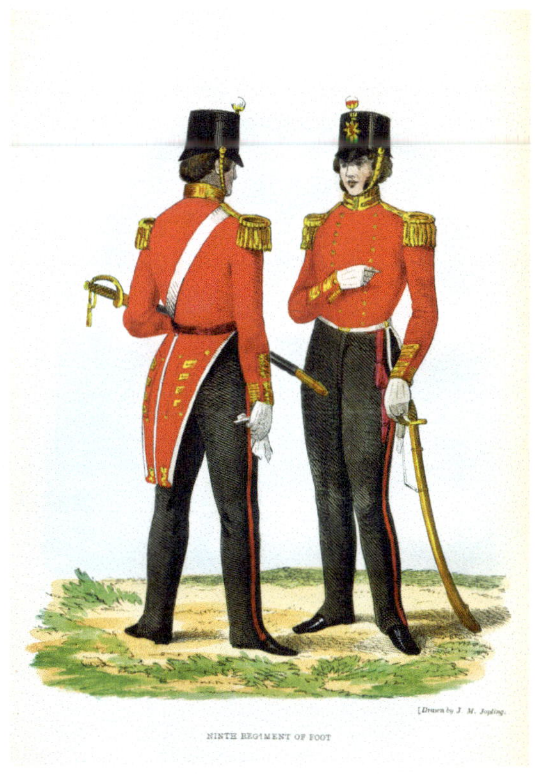

Officers uniforms of the 9th (East Norfolk) Regiment, *c.* 1850.

in six days and then fought the Battle of Ferozeshuhur on 21–22 December 1845. An even greater feat was achieved by some members of the regiment who marched the 320 miles with General 'Bobs' Roberts from Kabul to relieve besieged British forces at Kandahar in August 1880.

In 1881 the Childers Reforms restructured the British Army and the Ninth, or East Norfolk Regiment, was given its new official title of the Norfolk Regiment. Britannia Barracks was built 1886–87 by Norwich City Council on Mousehold Heath and presented to the Norfolk Regiment as its first permanent depot.

The last major actions of Queen Victoria's reign were fought during the South African War (1899–1902). Regulars of 2nd Battalion, the Norfolk Regiment and, for the first time, the 1st, 2nd, 3rd and 4th Volunteer Battalions and Volunteer Service Companies all saw active service. A number of Norfolk Regiment men served as Mounted Infantry (MI) – usually this can only be found out from their service papers. Medals named to Norfolk Regiment MI exist but are rare.

Under the Haldane Reforms (1906–12) the regular battalions of the Norfolk Regiment would alternate home service with duties around the empire. The new Territorial Force battalions were created from a core of selected members of the old Norfolk Volunteer Battalions (VB): the 4th Battalion drew its men from the 1st and 2nd VBs and the 5th Battalion from the 3rd and 4th VBs. Permission was also granted for the Norfolk Regiment to raise one of the eleven much vaunted Territorial cyclist battalions, which became 6th Battalion.

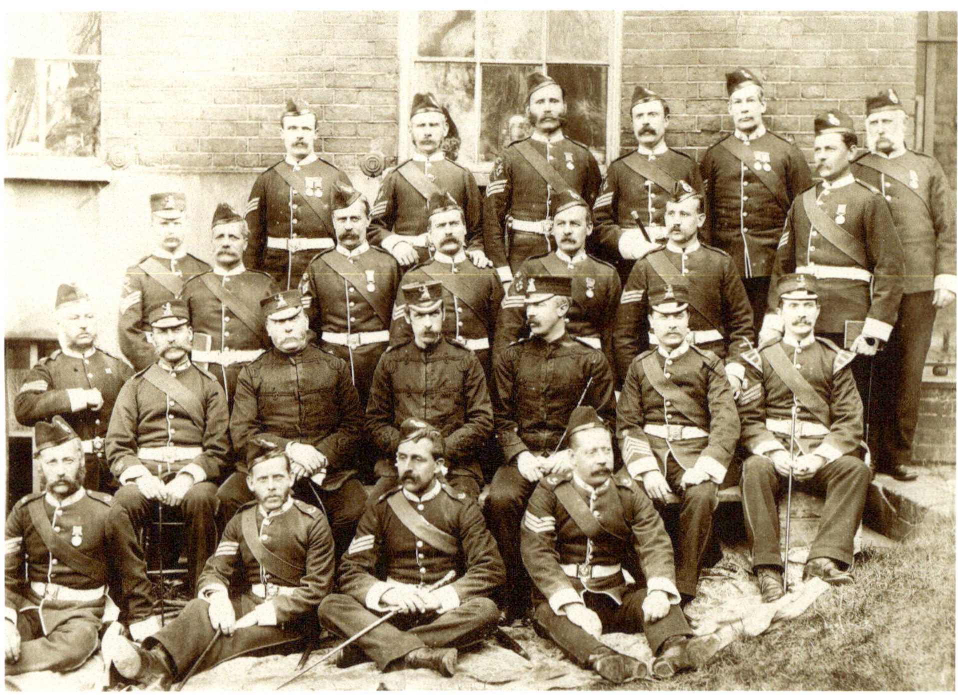

Officers and senior NCOs of the Norfolk Regiment Militia Battalion, c. 1895.

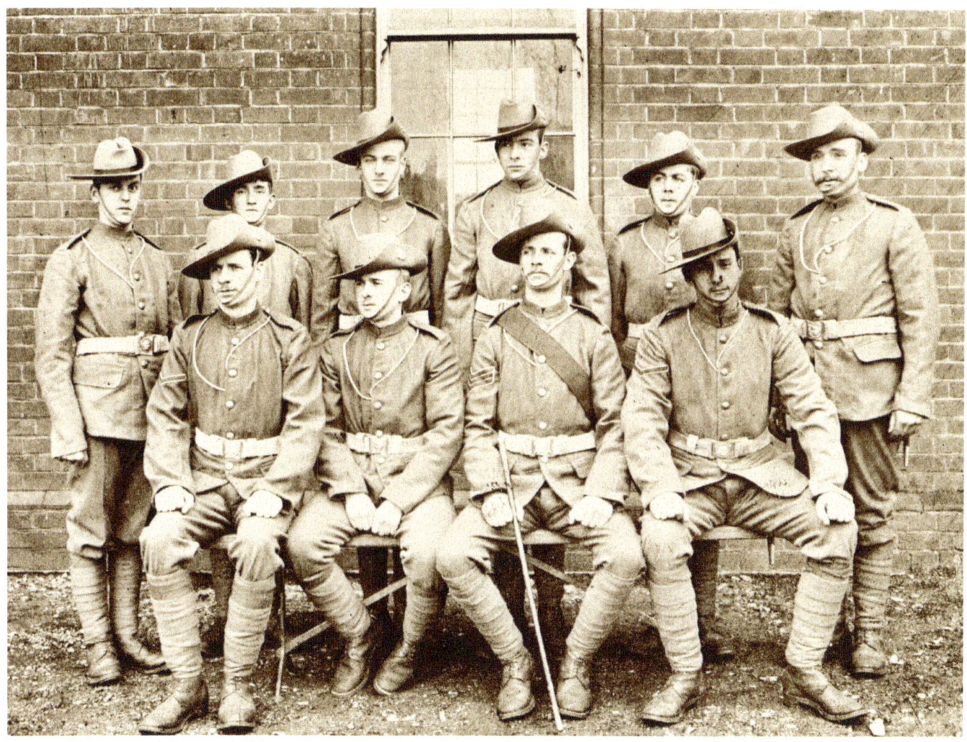

NCOs and men of 2nd Section, F Company, 2nd Volunteer Battalion, the Norfolk Regiment, shortly after their return to Great Yarmouth from serving in the South African War, 1902.

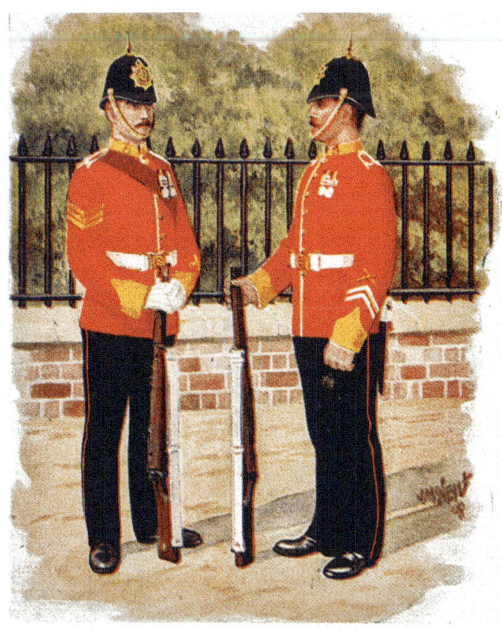

THE NORFOLK REGIMENT.

SOLDIERS' PAY.

INFANTRY.

After all stoppages for Messing and Washing have been deducted there remains for the Soldier to spend as he chooses :—

		s.	d.
WEEKLY.			
On joining		6	8¼
After two years' service (if proficient and serving on an approved term of more than three years) 2nd Class ...		8	5½
1st Class ...		10	2½

In addition to above, Lodging, Food, Fuel, and Medical Attendance are supplied free.

An allowance is given after 6 months' service to pay for replacing all articles of Kit and Clothing.

Men of good character are granted one month's Furlough annually, when they receive, besides the weekly sums mentioned in the table, an additional 5s. 6d. a week in lieu of the food ration.

Good soldiers permitted to continue in the Service for 21 years and upwards are entitled on discharge to Pensions for life varying from 1s. 1d. to 3s. 6d. per day provided that no service has been forfeited. A Warrant-Officer is entitled to a Pension of 4s. 6d. a day after 30 years' service.

A leaflet shewing terms of service, standards of height, age, &c., can be obtained at any Post Office or Barracks in the United Kingdom, or from any Recruiter.

God Save the King.

A Norfolk Regiment version of the Gale and Polden 'Soldiers' Pay' postcard, c. 1910.

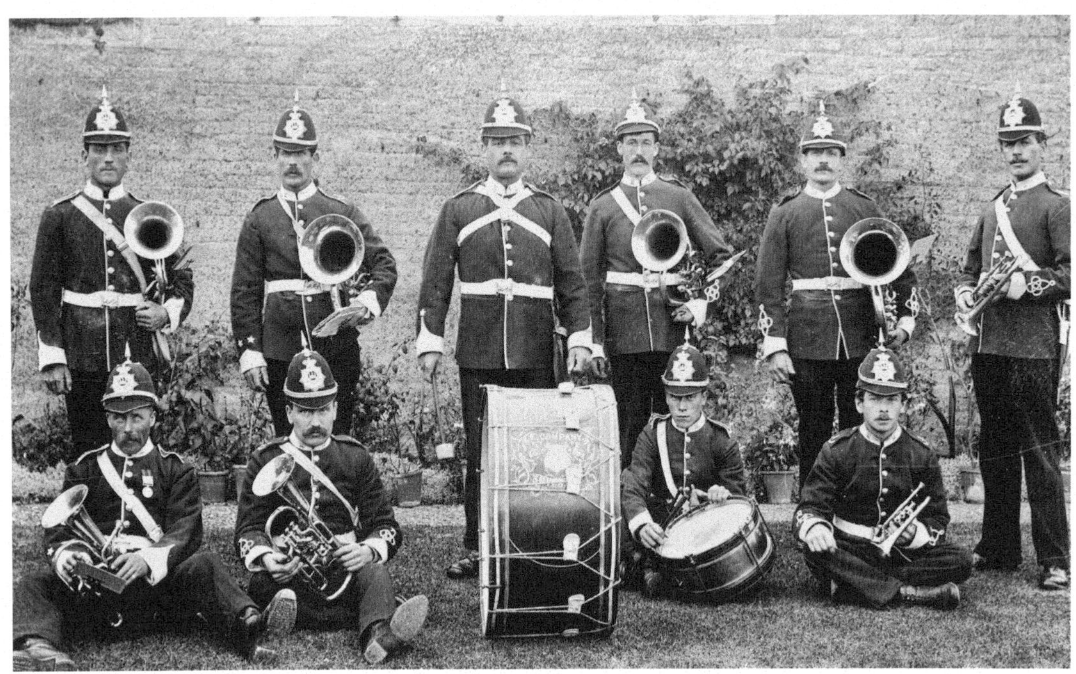

Bandsmen of E Company, 3rd Volunteer Battalion, the Norfolk Regiment, 1904.

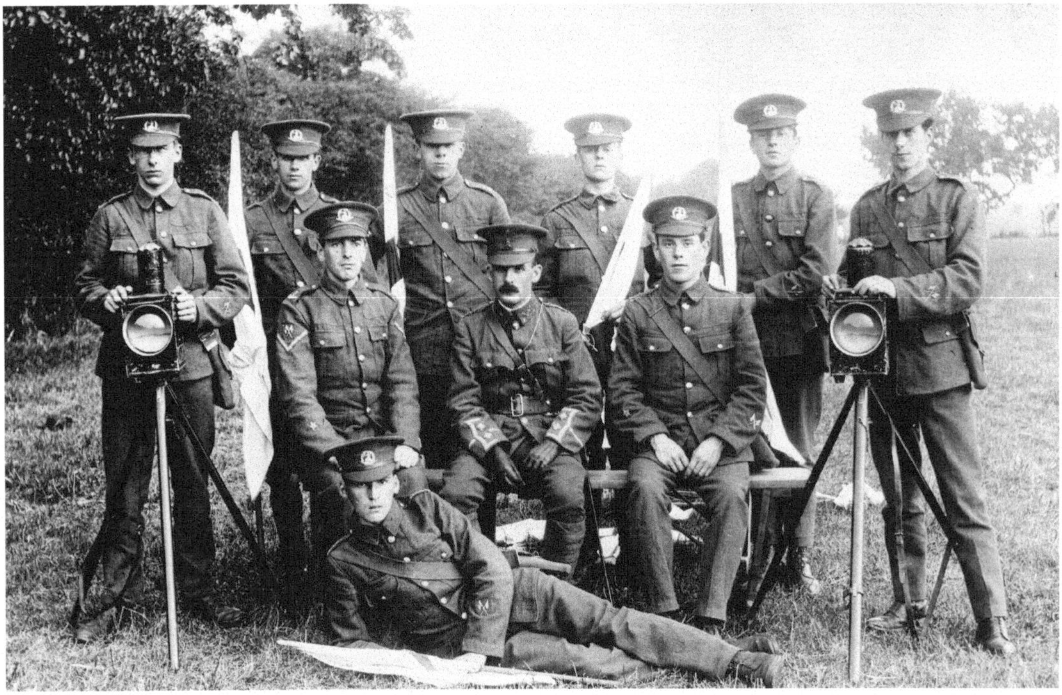

Signallers of HQ Company, 5th Battalion, the Norfolk Regiment, with their semaphore flags and Begbie signalling lamps, 1912.

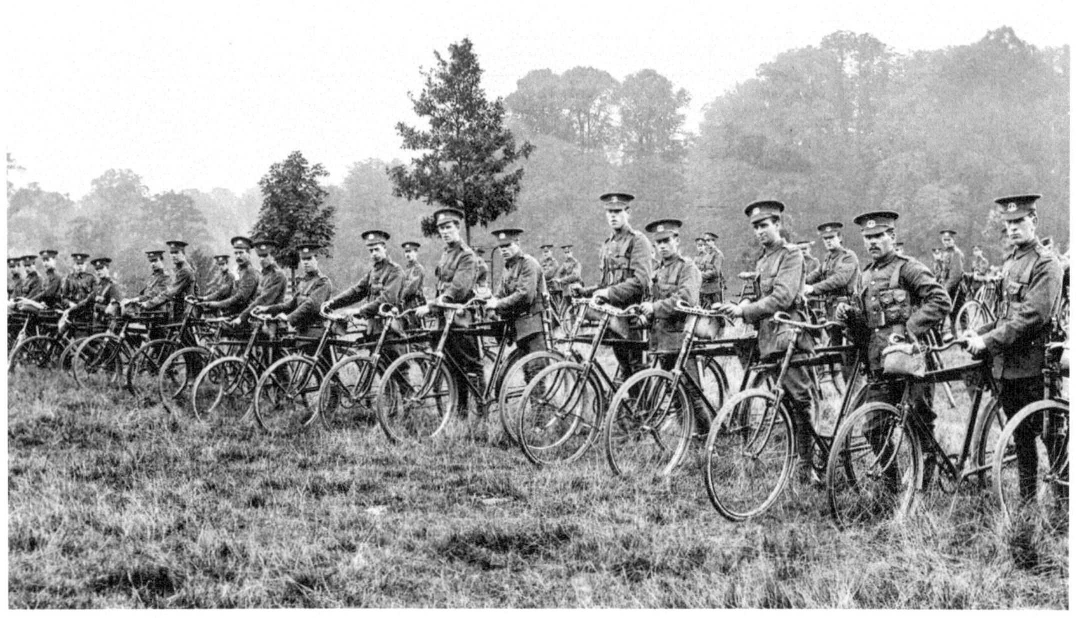

Members of 6th Battalion, the Norfolk Regiment (Cyclists) TF at Boughton Park Camp, 1913.

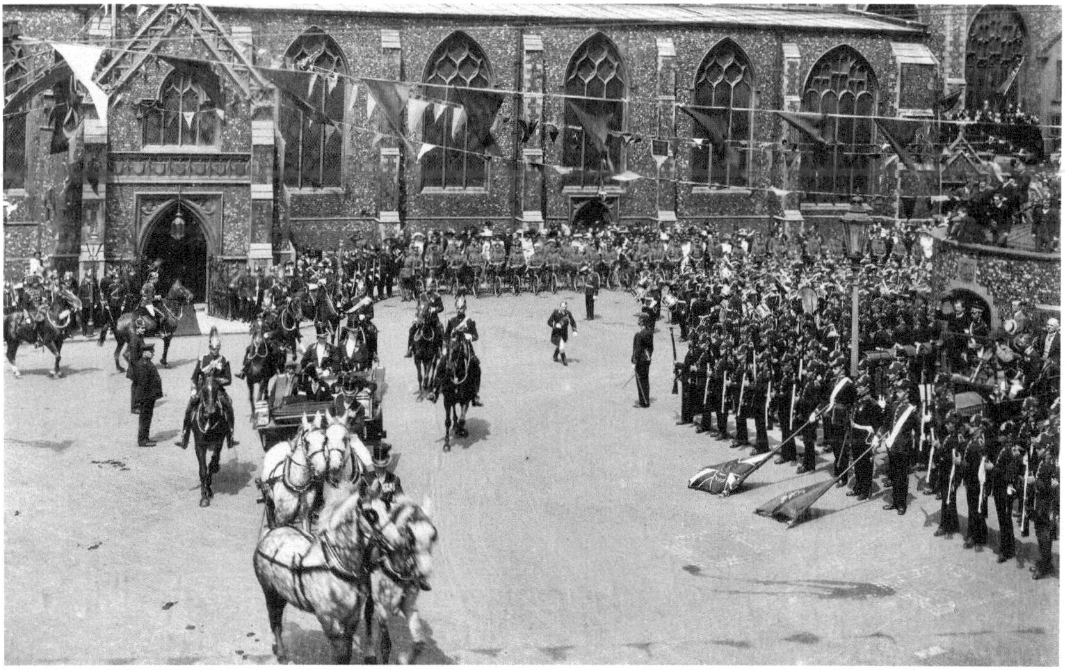

Colours of 4th Battalion dipped in salute as George V pulls away in his carriage from St Andrew's Hall during his first official visit to Norwich as king in 1911. The Norwich Company of 6th Battalion, the Norfolk Regiment (Cyclists) TF are also on parade. The king's mounted escorts were provided by the Norfolk Yeomanry.

First World War

When war broke out the two regular battalions of the Norfolk Regiment were on opposite sides of the world. The 1st Battalion were mobilised from Holywood, Ireland, and proceeded to France as part of the BEF in 1914. They spent the rest of the war on the Western Front, with only a brief departure to serve in the Italian campaign between November 1917 and April 1918 when they returned to the Western Front and fought on there until the end of the war.

Meanwhile the 2nd Battalion were out in their old garrison depot of Belgaum, India, when war broke out and were sent as part of 6th (Poona) Division to Mesopotamia in November 1914. They fought with great distinction at the Battle of Shaiba on 14 April 1915, but suffered terribly later on in the campaign during the Siege of Kut. On 29 April 1916, after 146 days of siege, Kut surrendered and the remnants of the 2nd Norfolks became prisoners of war, but that was not to be the end of the battalion. Initially they banded with the remaining men of the Dorset Regiment to form a composite battalion known as 'the Norsets'. Fresh drafts of men and recovered sick and wounded built up the ranks of 2nd Norfolk to become a battalion in its own right again. They fought fiercely, driving the enemy back along the Tigris, until the end of the war in 1918.

The 4th and 5th Battalions (Territorial Force) served as part of the East Anglian Brigade in the 54th Division out in Gallipoli, where the 5th Battalion sustained terrible casualties during an attack across Anafarta Plain on 12 August 1915. The battalions evacuated to Egypt in 1916 where they manned the Suez defences. When a new campaign opened in

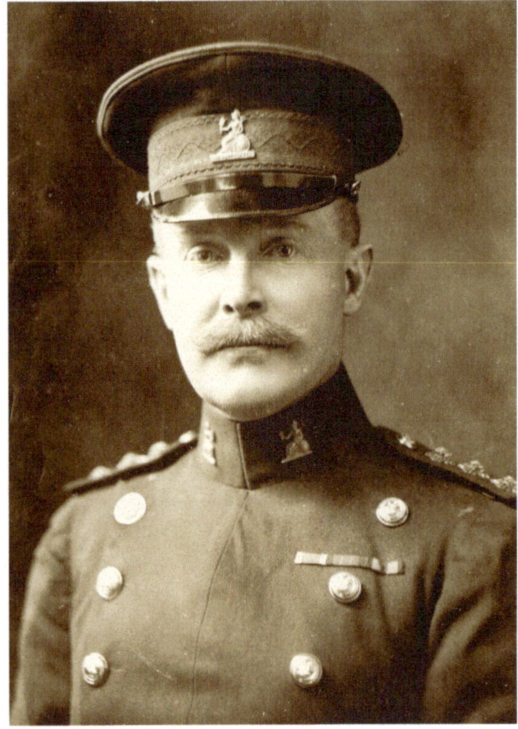

Major Charles Elmhurst Luard DSO, one of the first senior officer casualties of 1st Battalion, the Norfolk Regiment. He was last seen leading his company into action at Chivres Hill near Missy, Aisne, France, on 15 September 1914. Posted missing, presumed killed in action, he is commemorated on La Ferte-Sous-Jouarre Memorial.

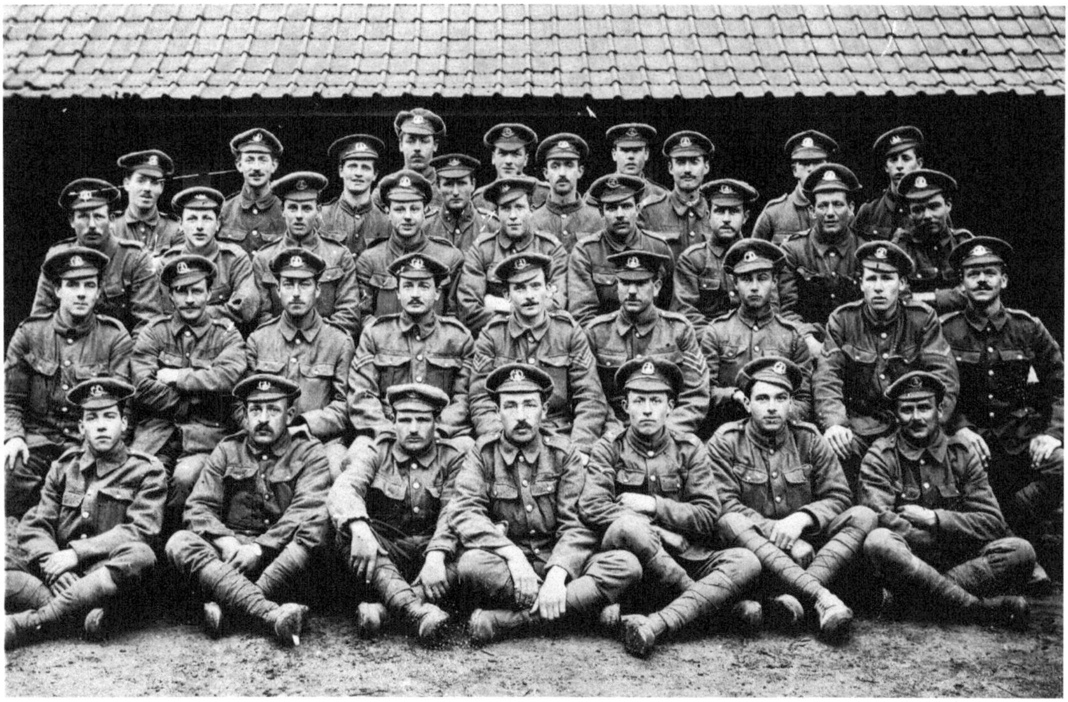

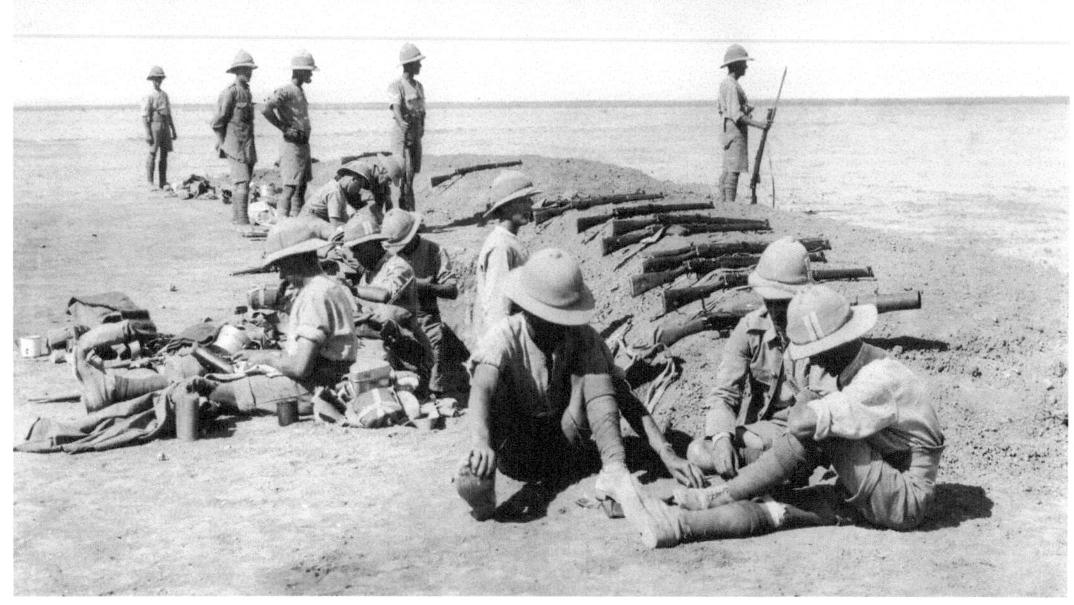

Men of 1st Battalion, the Norfolk Regiment (15th Brigade, 5th Division), 'Somewhere in France', May 1916.

Men of 2nd Battalion, the Norfolk Regiment (37th Infantry Brigade, 14th Indian Division) manning a front-line trench in the Jebel Hamarin, Mesopotamia, 1918.

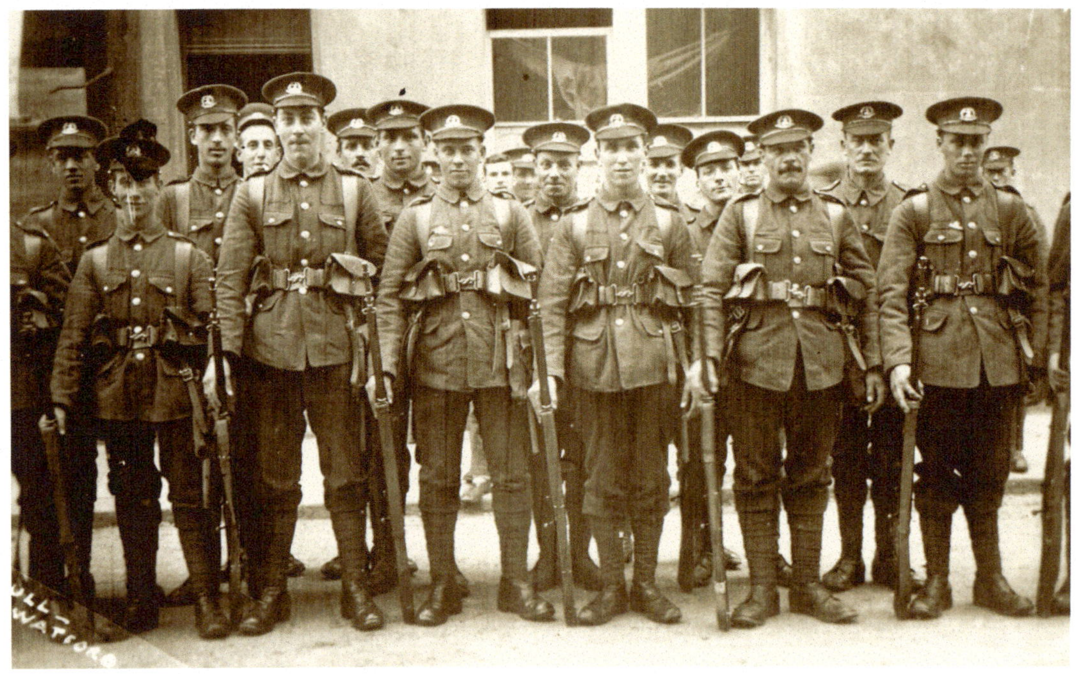

Men of 4th and 5th Battalions, the Norfolk Regiment on parade at Watford, a short while before their departure to Gallipoli in 1915.

Palestine the two territorial battalions crossed the Sinai Desert to join the fighting. Both battalions suffered severe casualties at the Second Battle of Gaza on 19 April 1917. The 6th Battalion (Cyclists) were deployed on coastal-defence duties from 1914, but were gradually depleted from 1915 as fit men were withdrawn for active service battalions on the Western Front. The remaining members of the battalion, bolstered by new recruits and conscripts, did eventually go overseas to Ireland on peacekeeping duties.

The three New Army battalions raised in Norfolk in 1914 were adopted as the 7th, 8th and 9th (Service) Battalions, the Norfolk Regiment, all of which were on active service in France by August 1915. All three battalions fought on the Ypres and Somme salients. The 8th (Service) Battalion went into action with 18th (Eastern) Division on the first day of the Somme on 1 July 1916. Their attack on Montauban was one of the few successes, but at a cost of four officers and 104 other ranks killed and over 200 wounded.

Every Territorial battalion raised a further two reserve battalions. The service battalions had the 10th Battalion, which supplied cadres of troops to the active service battalions of the Norfolk Regiment and other county regiments when they were in need of reinforcements. In total, over 5,500 officers and men of the Norfolk Regiment died and an estimated 25,000 were wounded during the First World War.

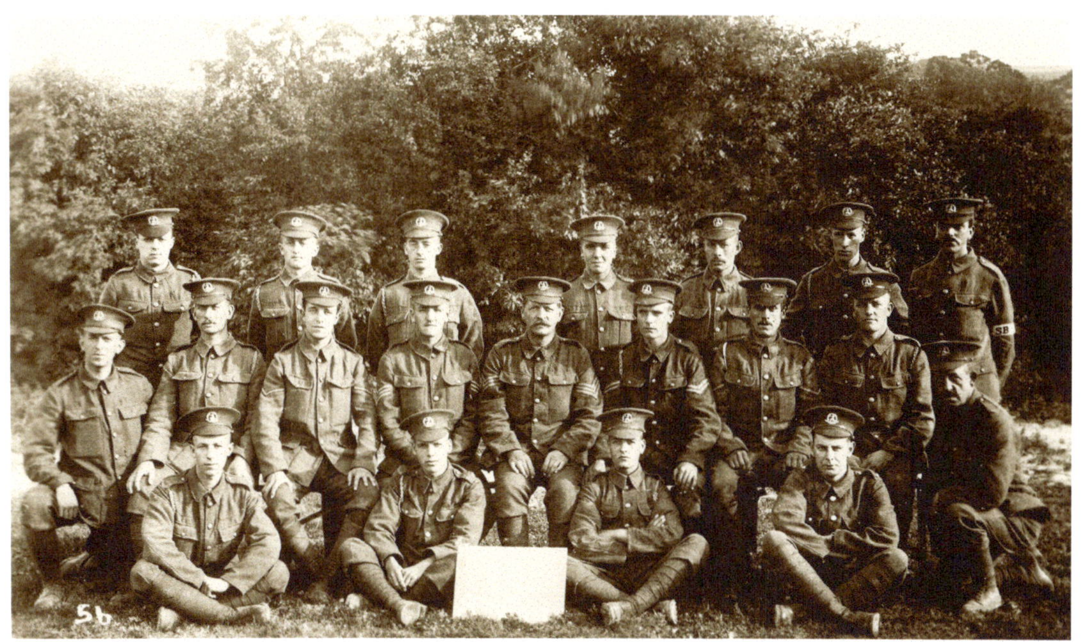

Men who answered Kitchener's call. Former staff of the Great Eastern Railway serving in 8th (Service) Battalion, the Norfolk Regiment, 1915.

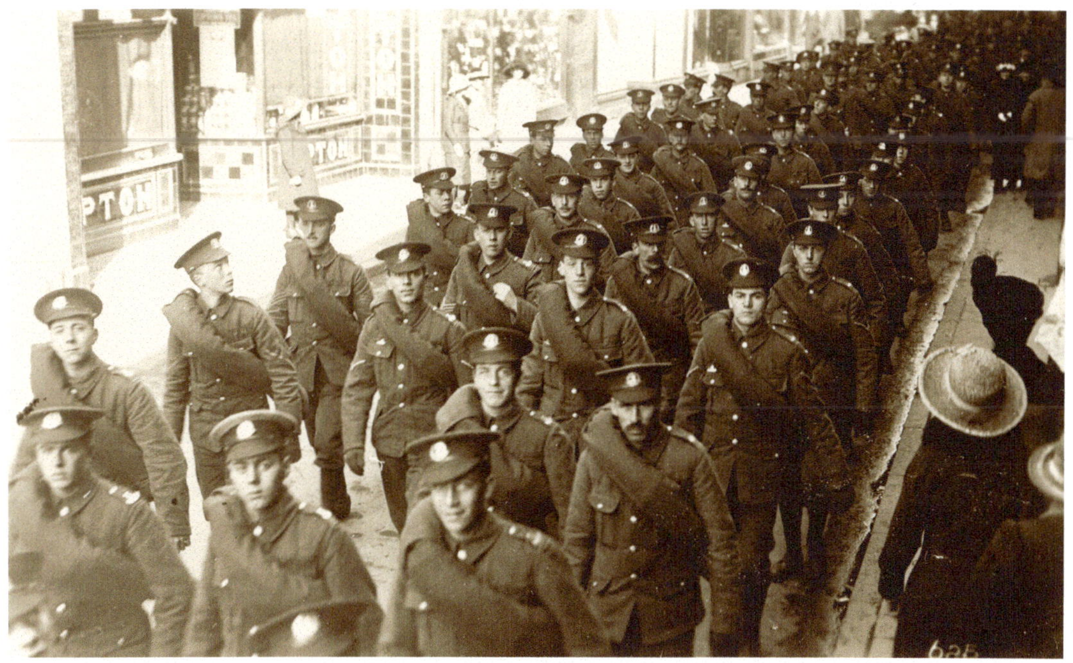

Arrival of 2/5th Battalion, the Norfolk Regiment at Peterborough in 1914.

Interwar Years

In 1923, 1st Norfolk embarked on its tour of foreign duties, first proceeding to the West Indies, then on to Egypt in 1925, Shanghai in 1928 and finally to India where it would serve throughout the 1930s, including a tour of duty along the north-west frontier. After

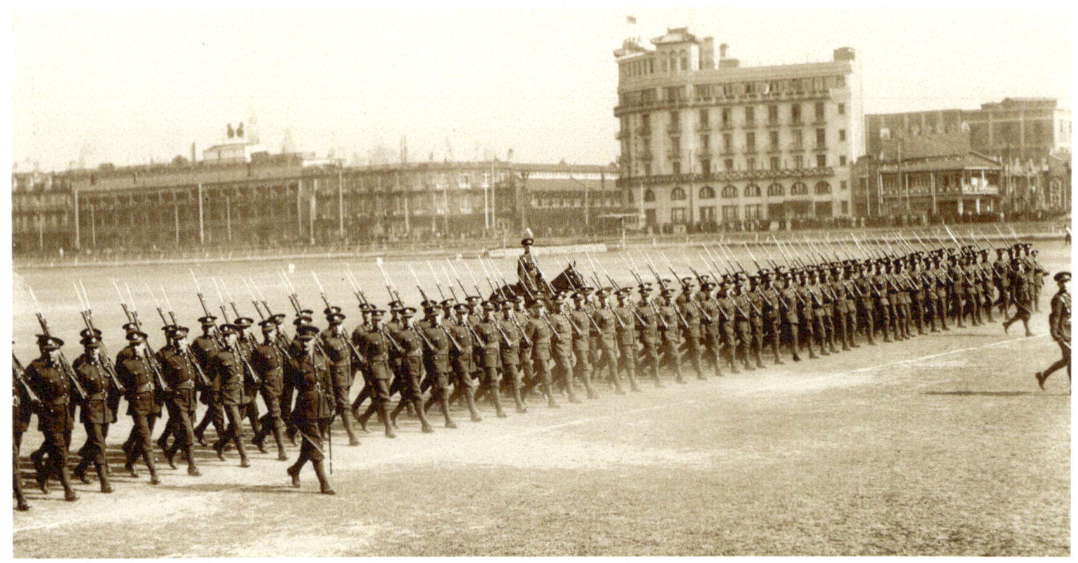

'Eyes right' – men of B Company, 1st Battalion, the Norfolk Regiment march past in general salute for the GOC North China in February 1929.

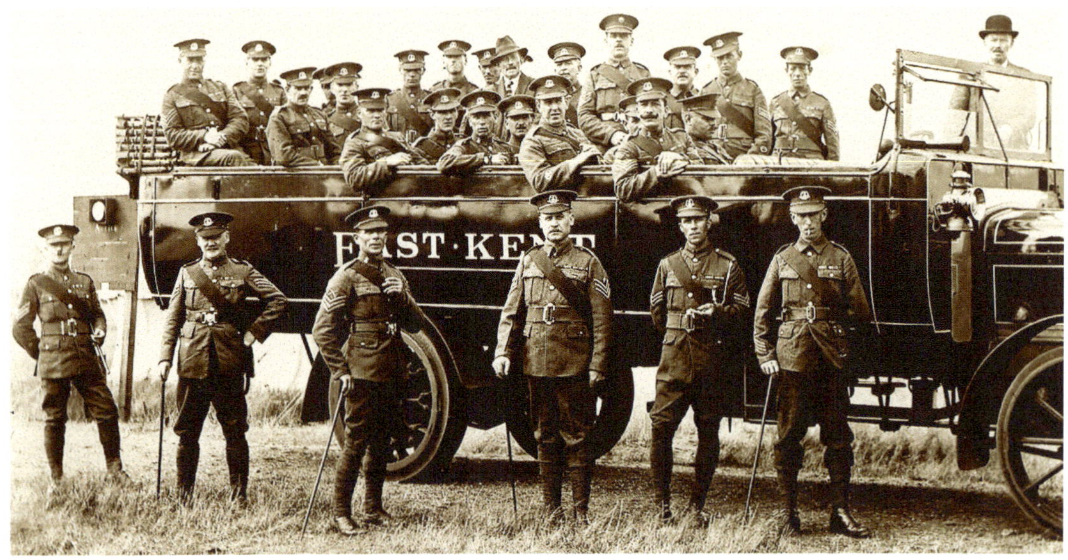

Senior NCOs of 4th Battalion, the Norfolk Regiment, off on a day trip to Dover from their summer camp at Swingate, 1935.

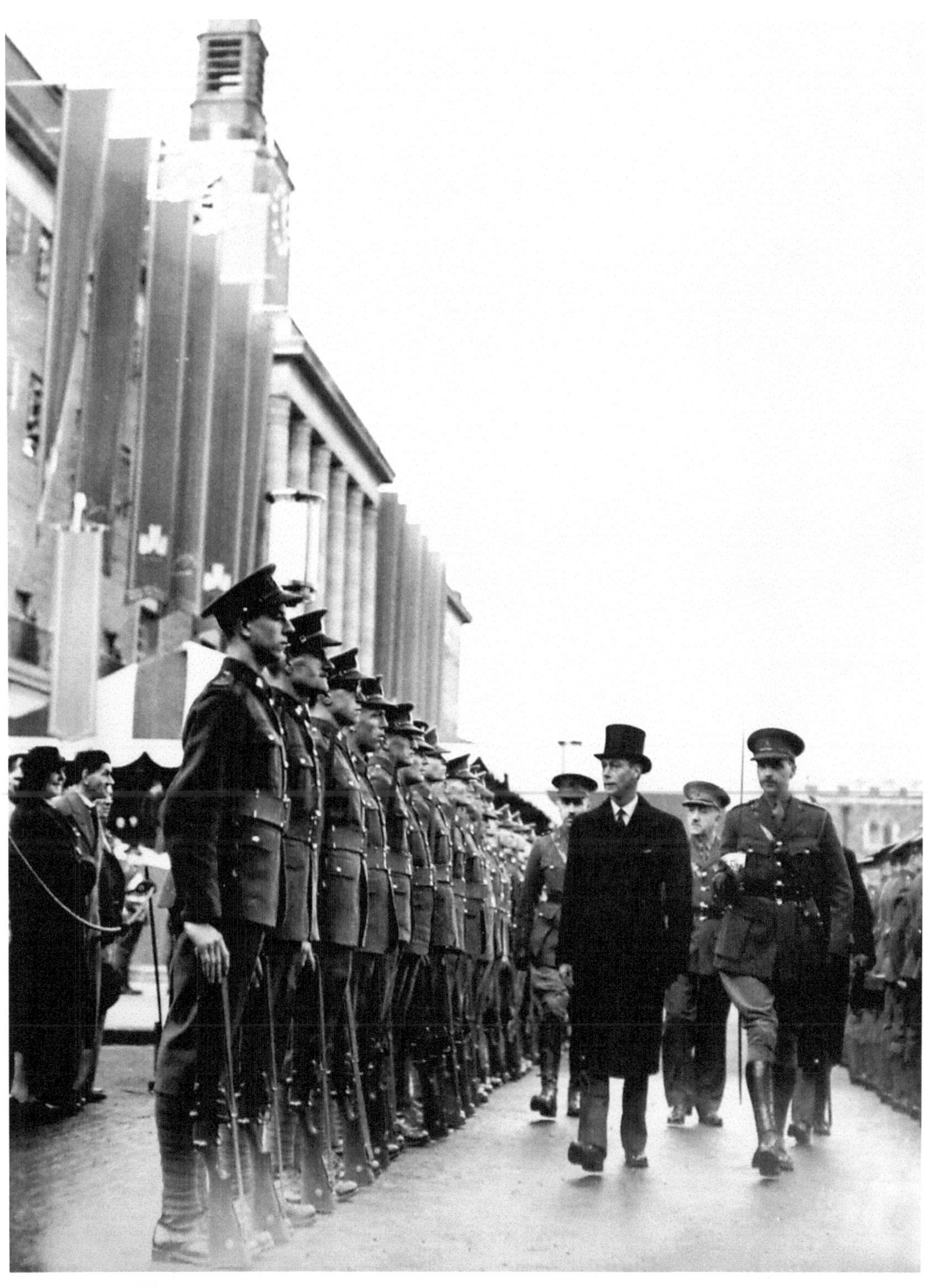

Guard of honour provided by men of 4th Battalion, the Royal Norfolk Regiment being inspected by George VI at the opening of the new Norwich City Hall on 29 October 1938.

engagement in the Waziristan campaign (1919–20) 2nd Norfolk finally returned to the UK in 1924 and entered home service at such bases as Colchester and Aldershot. The battalion only proceeded overseas again to Gibraltar in 1937 and returned again to England in January 1939.

The new TA battalions of the Norfolk Regiment were 4th Battalion, with headquarters at Norwich, and 5th Battalion at East Dereham. Throughout the 1920s and 1930s the training structure was similar to the pre-First World War years in that the recruit was put through his paces in drill and rifle, but with the addition of new weaponry such as machine guns and up-to-date mortars. New TA buildings were also erected, such as the new 5th Battalion HQ at East Dereham (1926) and the drill halls at Dersingham (1930), North Walsham (1933–34), King's Lynn (1936) and Methwold (1939). Many old soldiers looked back on this period as a 'golden age' of summer camps, sporting events and parades.

The interwar years also saw the Norfolk Regiment honoured by being made a 'Royal Regiment' for their distinguished service during the First World War on the occasion of the Silver Jubilee of George V in 1935, which also coincided with the 250th anniversary of the regiment. Full expansion of the TA was only ordered on the eve of war on 2 March 1939, when it was announced that the size of the TA was to be doubled. The expansion led to the creation of 6th and 7th Battalions, Royal Norfolk Regiment (TA).

The Second World War

The outbreak of the war on 3 September 1939 saw the regular army battalions of the Royal Norfolk Regiment in exactly opposite positions to those they were in at the outbreak of war in 1914. The 1st Battalion was out in India and this time it would be the 2nd Battalion that would become part of the British Expeditionary Force; indeed, they were the first complete infantry unit of the BEF to land in France. Members of the 2nd Royal Norfolk were awarded the first army decorations during the Second World War when Captain Peter Barclay and Corporal H. A. 'Mick' Davis were respectively granted the Military Cross and Military Medal for their gallantry during a scouting mission and subsequent contact with the enemy on the night of 3–4 January 1940. When Hitler unleashed Blitzkrieg in May 1940 the battalion became part of the rearguard for the BEF as they made for the evacuation beaches at Dunkirk. Their casualties were heavy and tragically over ninety men of the battalion were massacred by the SS after they surrendered at Le Paradis, France. Out of a unit of almost 1,000 men, just five officers and 134 other ranks of 2nd Royal Norfolk returned to Britain during the Dunkirk evacuation. The battalion was rebuilt and deployed to fight in India and Burma as part of the 2nd Division in April 1944. Just a month after their arrival they were plunged in at the deep end again on 4–6 May 1944 fighting in one of the bloodiest actions of the entire war in the Far East – the Battle of Kohima. They fought on and saw out the campaign to the end in 1945.

The first TA battalion of the Royal Norfolk Regiment to see action in the Second World War was the youngest of them all, the 7th Battalion who landed in France in January 1940. As the BEF were retreating, 7th Royal Norfolk were deployed in a planned counter-attack

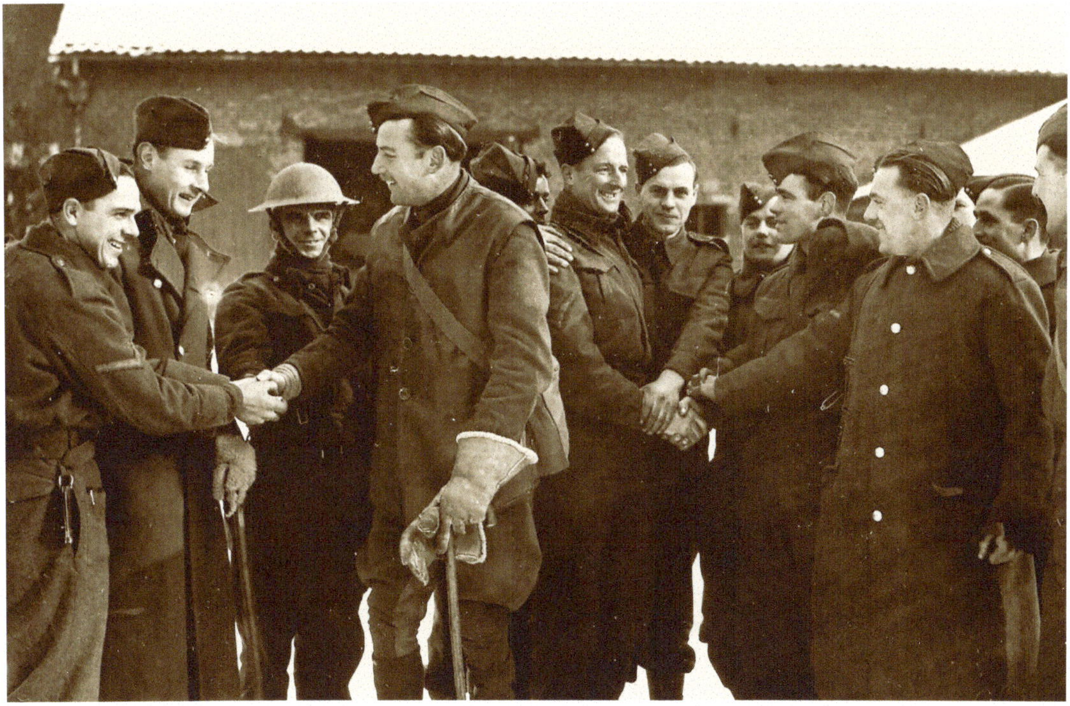

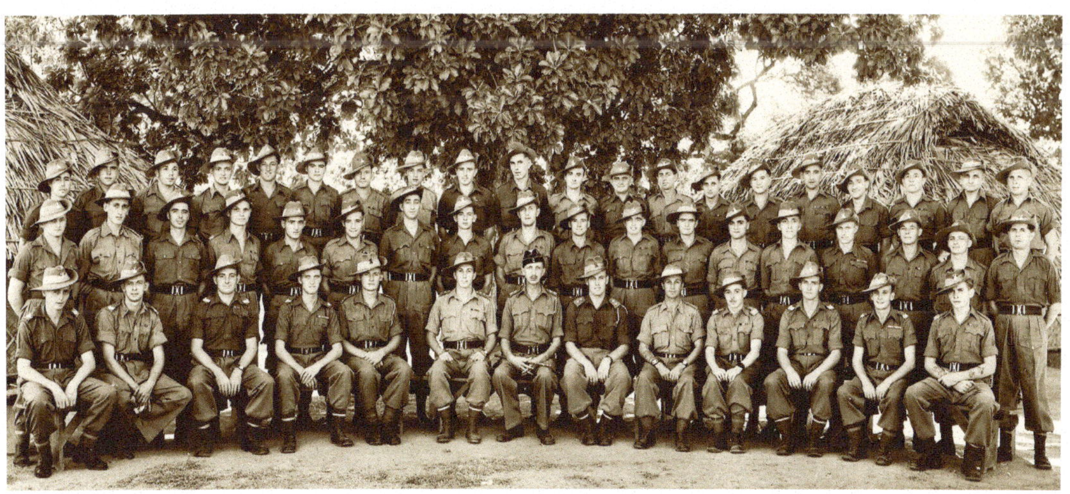

Captain Peter Barclay (left) and Lance Corporal 'Mick' Davies, 2nd Battalion, the Royal Norfolk Regiment, being congratulated by their comrades after the announcement the pair were to receive the first army gallantry decorations of the Second World War, 1940.

Officers and men from 2nd Battalion, the Royal Norfolk Regiment, India, 1945.

on Arras that ended, for the majority of the battalion, with either death or surrender at St Valery. Just twenty-nine other ranks and one officer (Lieutenant 'Lucky Jim' Walker) managed to get to a boat and escape out of the harbour back to England. The battalion would be raised again and as part of 176th Brigade, 59 Division, and landed in France again on 28 June 1944. The battalion fought bravely and doggedly at Epron and at the Orne River Crossing, but the losses were heavy and shortly afterwards they were disbanded and the remaining officers and men were sent as reinforcements to other units.

For the men of 4th, 5th and 6th Battalions, the Royal Norfolk Regiment TA, it was somewhat ironic that after weathering one of the coldest winters on record while manning coastal defences along the Norfolk coast in 1940 they should be deployed to Singapore, one of the hottest theatres of war in January 1942. Contrary to myth, they did not step off the boats into captivity. The men of the Norfolk TA battalions advanced to the straits of Johore and then fought bravely, defending Singapore Island alongside other local battalions in the 18th (Eastern) Division. The fighting was hard and the situation became desperate. The garrison could not hold out and senior commanders agreed terms of surrender on 15 February 1942. All three battalions were taken into captivity along with the rest of 18th Division, during which time most of them were forced to labour constructing the Burma–Siam Railway. Starved, beaten, tortured and denied proper food and medical care, hundreds of Norfolk lads died or were left with life-changing injuries at Japanese hands until they were liberated in September 1945.

After its return from India, 1st Royal Norfolk was sent to man the defences of London during the invasion scares of 1940. Hopes were high they might be deployed to North Africa, but they remained there until September 1942. It would only be after their transfer to the 3rd Division, 'the Iron Division', they began training as part of an assault division in Scotland in November 1943. April 1944 saw the end of the assault exercises in Scotland and the battalion left for the south of England.

One last series of practice landings – Exercise Fabius – was staged at Littlehampton in May, where the battalion made its final preparations before they departed as part of Operation Overlord. The 1st Royal Norfolk landed on Queen Red Sector of Sword Beach, Normandy, on 6 June 1944. They stormed up the beach in the second wave, but the so-called 'battle of the hedgerows' would prove far more costly as they advanced to Caen. The battalion fought with great distinction through the liberation of France, Belgium Holland and joined the final advance across the Rhine into Germany and victory in May 1945.

Members of the Royal Norfolk Regiment were awarded more Victoria Crosses than any other infantry regiment during the Second World War:

CSM George Gristock VC (Posthumous), River Escaut, Belgium, 21st May 1940
L/Cpl. Sidney Bates VC (Posthumous) Pavee, Sourdeval, France, 8th August 1944
Capt. David Auldjo Jamieson VC, Grimbosq, Orne Bridgshead, France, 7th-8th August 1944
Capt. John Niel 'Jack' Randle (Posthumous), Battle of Kohima, India, 6th May 1944
Lieut. George Arthur Knowland VC (Posthumous) Kangaw, Burma, 21st January 1945

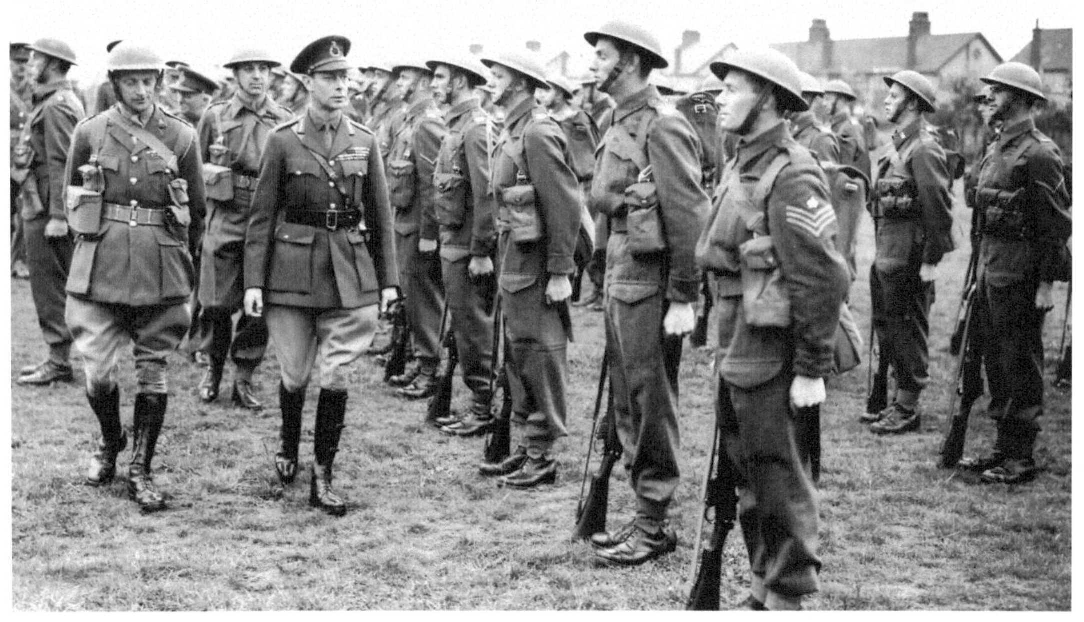

George VI inspecting men of 4th Battalion, the Royal Norfolk Regiment (TA) at Great Yarmouth racecourse, August 1940.

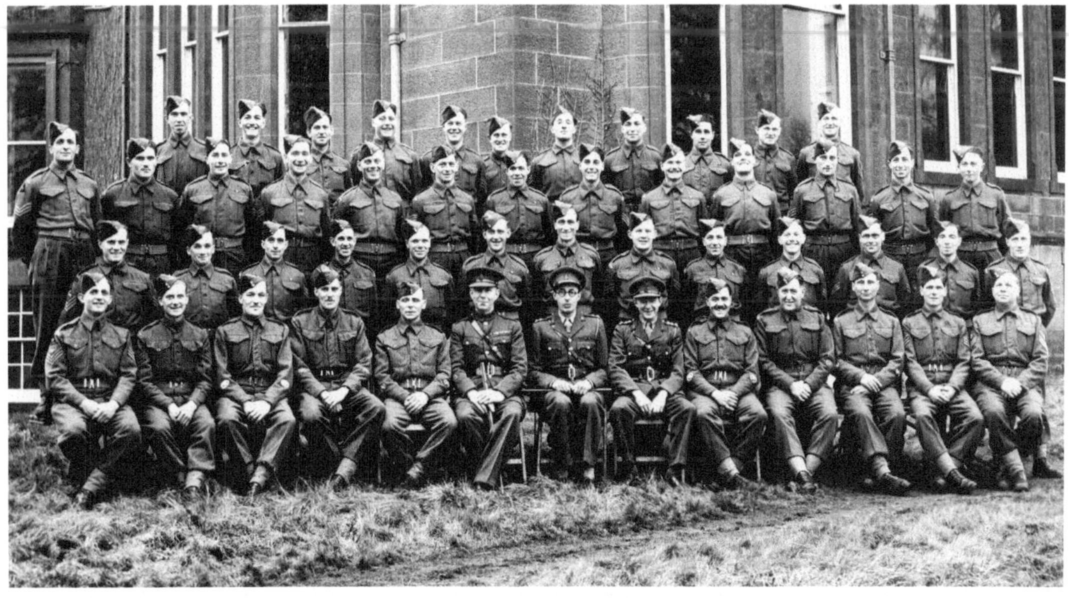

Sergeants' Mess, 1st Battalion, the Royal Norfolk Regiment, Halleaths, Dumfriesshire, Scotland, Christmas 1943.

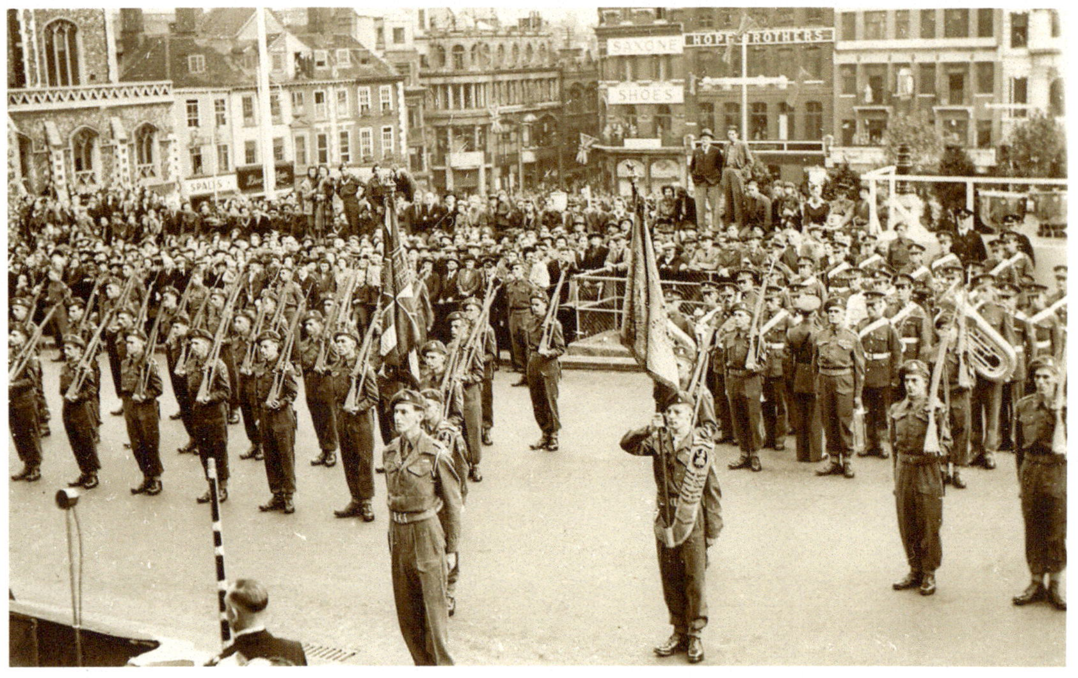

Representatives of all battalions of the Royal Norfolk Regiment on parade in front of City Hall to receive the Freedom of Norwich, 1946.

End of an Era

The Royal Norfolk Regiment fought in its last major conflict during the Korean War (1950–53). The Defence White Paper of 1957 restructured the British Army and many regiments were amalgamated over the following years, much to the chagrin of old soldiers who felt their old regiments should retain their old individual identities. The Royal Norfolk Regiment and the Suffolk Regiment were amalgamated to form 1st Battalion, East Anglian Regiment, in 1959 and further amalgamation with other East Anglian regiments occurred in 1964, creating the Royal Anglian Regiment.

Postscript

Today, the descendant regiments of the old Norfolk Regiment, Yeomanry and Territorial Corps are still going strong and, as regulars or army-reserve units, serve their country in war zones and on peacekeeping missions all over the world. Sadly the tangible links with their military past are fading away, especially as the veterans who remember serving under the old cap badges get fewer every year. Britannia Barracks ceased to be the depot of the county regiment and the buildings were handed over to units of the TA in September 1959. The TA moved out in 1967 and Norwich Prison took over the barracks site, with the exception of Cameron House, which continued to serve as the Royal Norfolk Regiment Museum, Royal Anglian Regiment HQ, Regimental Association and services administration offices. In 1990 the Regimental Museum was removed to the Shirehall, the offices relocated soon after and Britannia Barracks lost its final links with the military. In

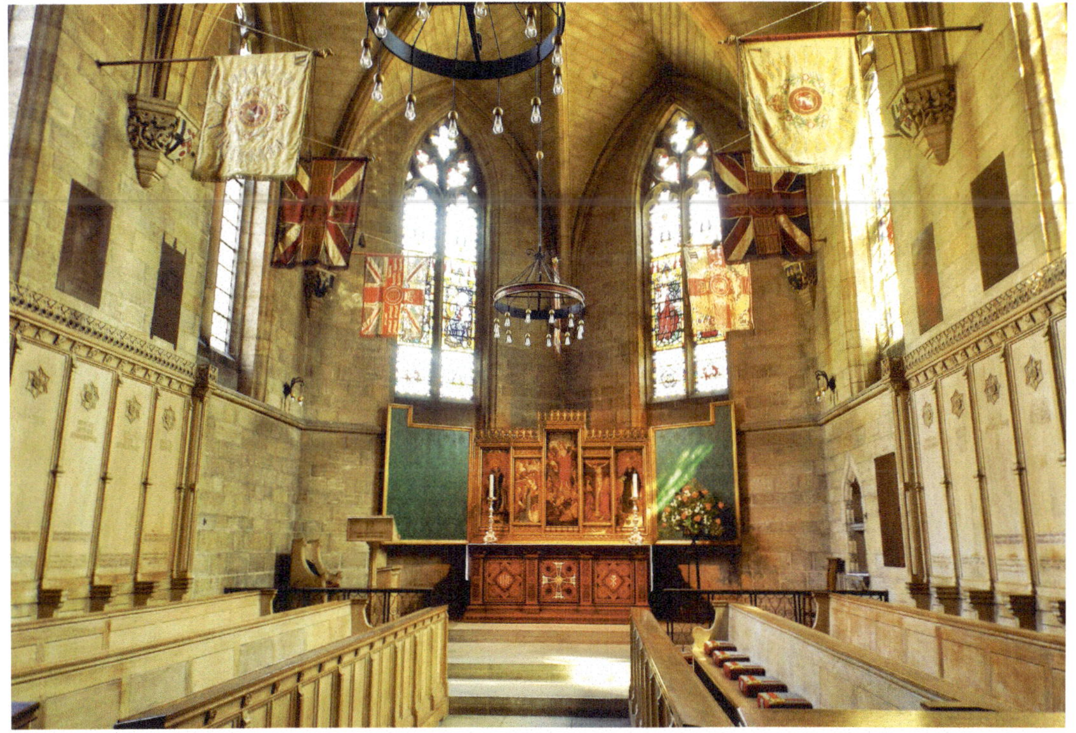

The Royal Norfolk Regimental Chapel at Norwich Cathedral, dedicated in 1958. It is a very fine place to see some of the laid-up colours of the regiment, the county rolls of honour and take time to remember the men of that noble old regiment.

recent years, however, the Britannia Cafe has opened in part of the old barracks building and its walls display memorabilia from its military past. The displays of the Regimental Museum are in the rotunda of Norwich Castle.

Norwich Cavalry Barracks did not fare so well. In the 1920s the barracks were initially taken over by the Royal Artillery and were renamed the Nelson Barracks. Used as an infantry training centre by a number of units, including the Royal Norfolk Regiment during the Second World War, the regular army handed the old barracks over to the Territorial Army for use as a training centre in 1947. It gradually fell into disuse and was finally demolished in 1965 and the majority of the site was used for social housing. Today there is next to no trace that a barracks ever existed on the site, save for a section of the old wall. In 1995 RAF Swanton Morley was handed over to the British Army and renamed Robertson Barracks. Used vy cavalry regiments such as the 9/12th Lancers and Light Dragoons, it was announced in 2016 that the barracks would close in 2031.

The majority of the USAAF bases in the county closed shortly after the end of the Second World War – the nearest now are Lakenheath and Mildenhall over the border in Suffolk. Even our RAF bases such as Neatishead and the famous Battle of Britain fighter airfield at Coltishall are now closed, but museums still exist on the sites. Only RAF Marham remains an active base today.

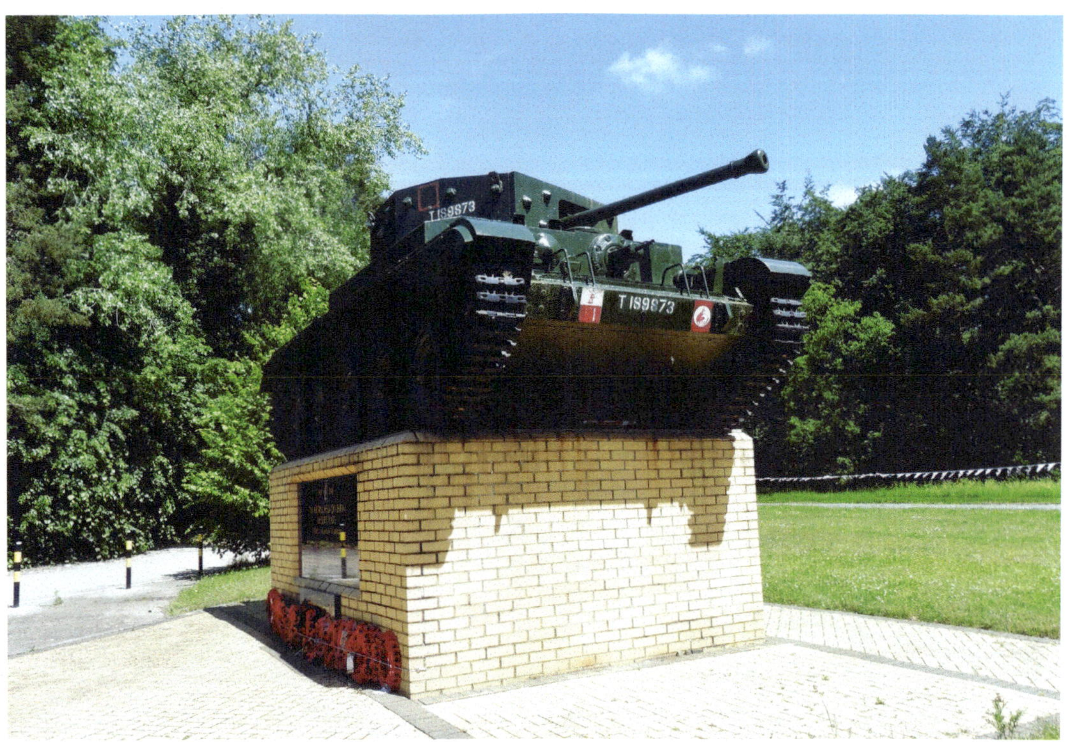

Mk IV Cromwell Tank, a replica of *Little Audrey*, 5 Able, B Squadron, 1st Royal Tank Regiment, memorial to the Desert Rats, Thetford Forest, inaugurated by Field Marshal Lord Carver on 23 October 1998.

Thetford and the Brecks have been a regular training area for local TA soldiers since the early twentieth century. At High Ash Camp in Thetford Forest, the 7th Armoured Division, the famous 'Desert Rats', fresh from their victories in the desert, spent January to May 1944 in training for their next deployment – Operation Overlord. It proved to be the only time the division was in the UK during the war. A Mk IV Cromwell Tank, a replica of *Little Audrey*, 5 Able, B Squadron, 1st Royal Tank Regiment was placed on a plinth with a memorial plaque to these men. The memorial was inaugurated by Field Marshal Lord Carver on 23 October 1998 and annual services and events have been held there ever since.

In 1940, 118,000 acres of this land on the Norfolk-Suffolk border was requisitioned by the War Office for manoeuvres without live firing. This area included the villages of Buckenham Tofts, Langford, Stanford, Tottington and West Tofts, and the villagers and farmers that were evacuated to other areas. After the war many felt very bitter because they had been told that when the war was over they would return to their homes, but this did not happen. In 1942, 16,000 acres of the land became a specific battle area suitable for combined operations training and a 'Nazi village' was created for soldiers to learn the skills for fighting in built-up areas. In 1950, 27,000 acres were purchased to create a permanent 'Principal Training Area' at Stanford. In 2009, STANTA had a replica Afghan village constructed over a 12.5-acre site complete with a market and a mosque for the training of troops. Today, STANTA covers a total of 30,000 acres and is still used for the training of both artillery and infantry units of the regular army and army reserve, as well as cadets.

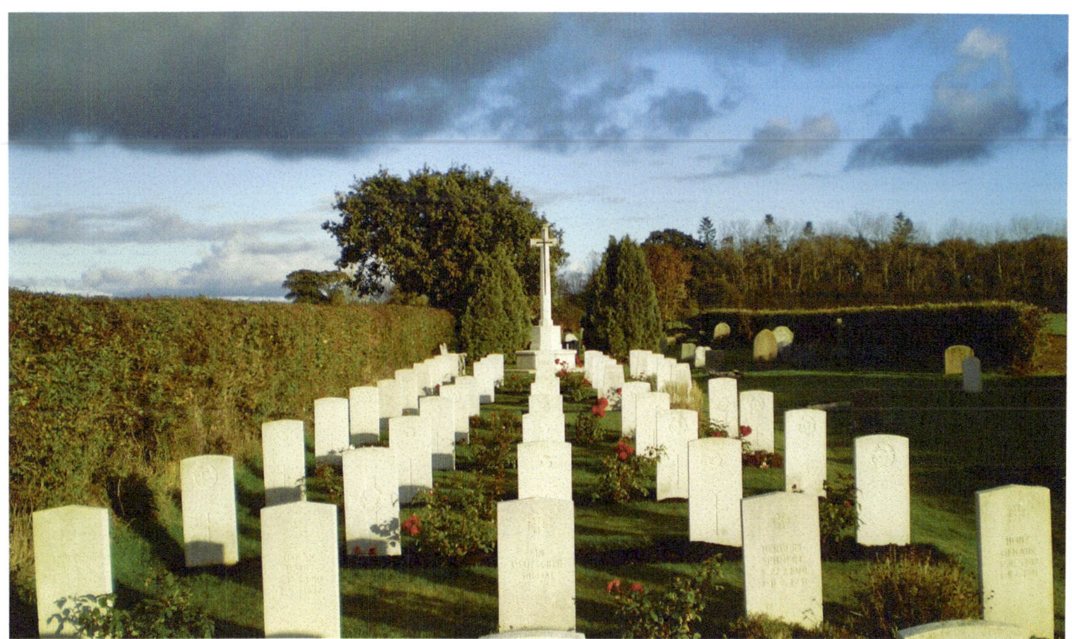

The Commonwealth War Graves Cemetery at Scottow. Built for the dead of RAF Coltishall, the fifty-four graves here from the Second World War remind us that those who served came from all over the world for there are aircrew buried here from Czechoslovakia, Australia, New Zealand, Canada and even Germany.

Acknowledgements

The author would like to record his personal thanks to the following for their kind assistance with this book and over his years of research: John Fielding for his excellent aerial photographs of the ancient fortifications, Major Gary Walker, Captain John Lincoln, the late John Slaughter, Stewart P. Evans, Bronwen Tyler, Kate Thaxton, the Royal Norfolk Regimental Museum, Norwich Cathedral, Norfolk and Norwich Heritage Centre, Norfolk Record Office, BBC Radio Norfolk, and last – but no means least – thanks to my partner Fiona Kay and our friends Lieutenant Colonel Martin Valles and his wife Kim for travelling a good few of the miles researching this book with me.

Printed and bound by CPI Group (UK) Ltd, Croydon, CR0 4YY

30/04/2026

02100290-0014